ARTS OF
RUSSIA

ARTS OF RUSSIA

From the Origins to the End of the 16th Century

KIRA KORNILOVICH

Translated from the Russian by James Hogarth

57 illustrations in colour

51 illustrations in black and white

NAGEL PUBLISHERS GENEVA PARIS MUNICH

PUBLISHER'S NOTE

The preparation of our various publications on Russia had drawn our attention to the lack of any general study of the history of Russian art; and the present work is designed to fill that gap. This first volume, which covers the period from the origins to the end of the 16th century, will shortly be followed by a second volume devoted to the 16th and 17th centuries.

We need not stress the difficulty of collecting illustrative material on the artistic work produced throughout the vast extent of Russian territory; and we are correspondingly grateful to all those who have assisted us in our arduous quest and have played a part, in either a private or an official capacity, in making possible the production of this work.

In the first place we should like to thank Mr V. A. Ankudinov, President of the Directorate of Foreign Tourism attached to the Council of Ministers of the U.S.S.R., who used the high authority of his office to give us every possible assistance.

Our gratitude is also due to Mr B. Piotrovsky, Director of the Hermitage Museum, to Mrs V. Berezina and Mr V.G. Lukonin, Keepers in that Museum, for much helpful advice.

We should also like to thank M. B. Lossky, Conservateur of the Musée National du Château de Fontainebleau, for his valuable assistance.

Finally our thanks are due to Mr V. Komolov, Director of Publications of the Novosti Press Agency, and to Messrs Shavranov and W. Tschan for their kindness in supplying us with illustrations.

In the first millennium A.D., in that distant time before there was any thought of an entity called the Russian people, the territory which was later to be the land of Rus or Russia was occupied by numerous tribes of Eastern Slavs who lived by hunting, fishing and to some extent by farming. Archaeological investigation has shown that they also possessed the rudiments of the art of building, for excavation has brought to light the remains of ancient settlements surrounded by earthen ramparts and stout timber palisades. (It is significant that the Russian word for town, *gorod*, originally meant an enclosed settlement).

In the construction of their simple dwellings these Slavonic tribes used a variety of materials. In the Dnieper area, for example, the houses were usually built in pisé; in the forest regions of the north-east they were of timber. (Here again we find echoes of the past in the Russian language: for example *zodchy*, an architect, comes from the Slavonic word for clay, and *plotnik*, a carpenter, comes from the word for a raft of logs).

The Slavs were pagans; and, as with other pagans, their gods were incarnations of the forces of nature and the elements who controlled the destinies of men and presided over all forms of human activity. The chief deities in the Slavonic pantheon were Dazhdbog the sun god (also known as Svarog or Khors or Yarila, for different tribes gave him different names); the god of the Winds, Stribog; Perun the Thunderer; the Earth Goddess; and Mokosh, the goddess of water. The Slavs also worshipped Radunitsa the goddess of spring and the patron divinities of love, the eternally youthful Lada and Lel. Indeed the list of their divinities is endless, for every corner of the visible world was peopled with a host of minor gods and spirits. The house was the domain of the diminutive house-demon; wells were inhabited by the well-sprite, rivers and lakes by the *rusalka* or water-nymph; in the forests lived the

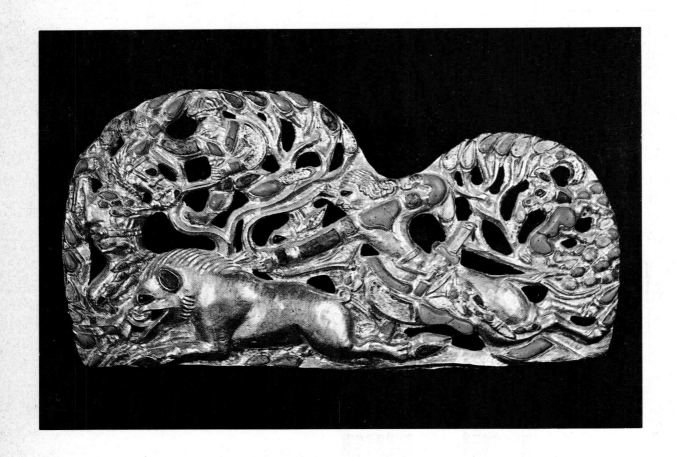

wood-demon; and the tracks used by animals and even the roads trodden by humans were haunted at night by Kashchey the Deathless and the nightmare hag Baba-Yaga who flew through the air in a mortar propelled by a pestle.

We know that the Slavs made sculptured representations of their divinities. The wooden statues which are mentioned by the chroniclers have not survived, but archaeologists have found a number of small figurines, both male and female, made of bronze, pottery or stone. Some of the stone images were of considerable size. All these works, however, are extremely primitive.

These statues were set up in sacred groves, and probably also in temples. The chronicler, at any rate, refers to "idols' houses" or shrines. We have some evidence about the Slavs of the Baltic area which indicates that these shrines were built of timber. Of building in stone we have so far only a single example—the remains of an oval structure built in grey sandstone which were found during excavations in the oldest part of Kiev in 1908. Most scholars agree in regarding this as a pagan temple.

The material which has come down to us in greatest quantity from this period consists of artefacts such as domestic utensils, weapons, and ornaments in great variety *(Plates pp. 8,9,11,12)*. Perhaps only the articles in this last group, however, can be regarded as works of art. They include buckles and

pendants—often made in the form of grotesque schematic figurines of animals and humans—as well as necklaces, bracelets and rings: all the trifles, in fact, which from time immemorial down to our own day have beguiled the vanity of men and women. Occasionally we find objects cast in silver, which are sometimes gilded, but usually they are made of bronze, stone or glass; the glass is sometimes gilded or coloured with metal oxides.

The great bulk of these articles were found during the excavation of funerary *kurgans* (earthen mounds erected over the remains of the dead). There is nothing surprising about this. The ancient Slavs shared the general pagan belief in a life beyond the grave which was similar in all respects to life on earth. Accordingly they took with them into the grave all that they had loved during their earthly existence and would need in their future life—their wife, their favourite horse, their weapons, their household goods. The dead man was clad in his finest raiment, his "wedding garments". Nothing less than this was conceivable, for when he appeared before the immortal gods he must present himself in all the magnificence he had enjoyed in life.

The artistic culture of the Eastern Slavs was the infancy of Russian art, but it prepared the ground for the later flowering of that art. The rapid development in ancient Russia of timber building, decorative woodcarving and metalworking was the result of many centuries' experience in the carpenter's craft, in carving and in metalworking, including the handling of precious metals. Many of the patterns created by these early craftsmen, in which a complex design of vegetable motifs and scrollwork is curiously combined with schematic representations of human beings and animals—varied in the course of time and enriched by new themes—have remained as basic elements in the repertoire of Russian ornament. They were common in folk art at the beginning of the 20th century, and are still found even in our own day in painting, woodcarving and above all in embroidery.

II KIEV, MOTHER OF RUSSIAN CITIES

The irresistible advance of history sweeps away everything in its path. In due course the tribal system, with its patriarchal way of life, passed into limbo; and at the end of the 9th century and in the 10th the first Russian feudal state, the Princedom of Kiev, grew up on the ruins of the older world.

A new social order now came into being and made its influence felt in many directions. The land increasingly fell into the hands of large proprietors, and the gulf between rich and poor, between the nobility and the ordinary people, became ever wider. The artistic life of the princedom now developed in the towns, which steadily increased in number: at the end of the 9th century there were twenty-five, by the end of the 11th century two hundred. The development of a class structure in society determined the character of building in these towns: side by side with the hovels of the craftsmen and the poorer classes stood the substantial dwellings of the more prosperous citizens and the handsome mansions of the princes and boyars.

The oldest Russian towns were Kiev, Chernigov and Novgorod; and in the 10th and 11th centuries Kiev occupied a position of particular importance and, as the capital of the princedom and the place where the Grand Prince held his court, was well named the "mother of Russian cities".

The origin of the name Kiev is unknown, and even the early Russians themselves were unable to decide what it meant. The chronicler, anxious to remain impartial, records two traditions current in his time. The first of these had it that Kiev was named after one Ky, a ferryman on the Dnieper. Alternatively it was thought that the city had been founded by three brothers, the Princes Ky, Shchek and Khoriv, along with their sister the Princess Lybed, and was named after the eldest of the brothers. The memory of the beautiful Princess Lybed is preserved in the placid stream of this name which flows into the Dnieper at Kiev.

Kiev stood on the great water route which ran "from the Varangians to the Greeks"—that is, from the Baltic to the Black Sea—and accordingly it soon developed into an important trading and cultural centre. The hoards of coins found in the Dnieper area bear witness to long-standing commercial relations with Byzantium and the countries of the East, and archaeological discoveries have provided evidence of the flourishing artistic production of the city.

The conversion of Russia to Christianity in the year 988 strengthened the political authority of the Kievan kingdom, for the introduction of a single unitary religion contributed to the rapid unification, "under the right hand of the Grand Prince", of the tribal lands which had hitherto been parcelled out among many owners. Moreover in accepting Christianity Russia became a full member of the family of European nations, able not only to enter into trading agreements with them but to make military and dynastic alliances; and these wider relationships were accompanied by a lively cultural interchange.

The acceptance of the new faith also led to a fundamental change in the character of Russian art. The first stone-built churches decorated with mosaics and frescoes made their appearance, and the art of icon-painting (in tempera on wood, the earliest form of easel-painting in Russia) began to develop.

This flowering of art in the Kievan kingdom took place during the reigns of Prince Vladimir (980-1015) and Prince Yaroslav the Wise (1019-1054). In this period Kiev's profusion of churches, the sumptuousness of their interiors, and the luxury of the Grand Prince's court impressed not only the half barbarous inhabitants of the steppes but also travellers from other countries who had some experience of the world. Thus Dietmar of Merseburg assures us that he had counted eight market-places and over four hundred churches in Kiev. Even though the latter figure may be somewhat

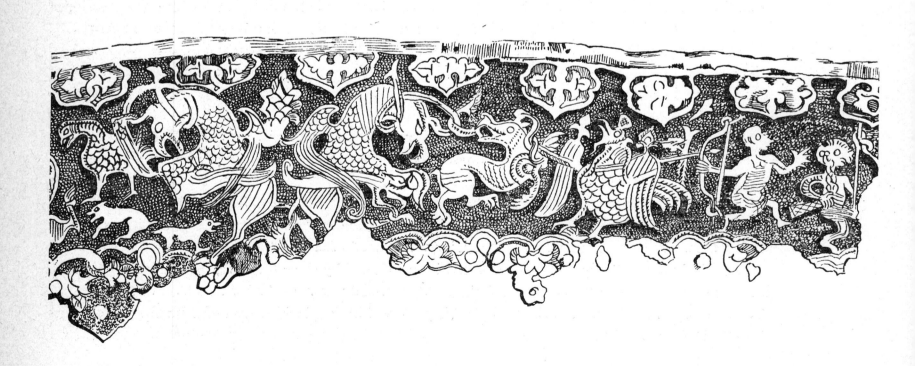

16

exaggerated, Dietmar's account gives us some idea of the impression produced even on a seasoned traveller by the earliest capital city of Russia.

If by some chance we found ourselves in Kiev as it was at the end of the 10th century and in the 11th, we should certainly lose our way in the densely packed maze of semi-underground huts in which the craftsmen and poorer classes of the town had their dwellings, clustering against the town ramparts and from there extending up the hill in a sea of green turf-covered roofs. Here and there a few timber buildings would stand out from the rest and the domes of churches would soar into the sky, and from place to place the houses would draw aside to make room for a market-place in which the craftsmen's wares and foodstuffs of all kinds were displayed for sale.

On the summit of the hill was the Prince's citadel, the architectural centre of Kiev. Within its walls were a church and the Prince's residence with his private apartments and audience chambers, in which "gracious Prince Vladimir, the Bright Sun" and his knights, raising beakers full of foaming mead, took counsel together on how best to defend the land of Rus against the hordes of the Heathen Idol or the foul serpent Tugarin. All this we learn from the *byliny*, the ancient epic poems of Russia. The chroniclers, too, tell of the Prince's residence with its golden domes and spacious audience chambers. In the square in front of the palace stood a bronze quadriga (four-horse chariot), which Vladimir had brought from Korsun (Chersonesus), and marble statues of goddesses of classical antiquity; and the square accordingly came to be known as the Women's Market.

The Desyatinnaya Church in Kiev was the first stone-built church in Russia. It was the work of Byzantine craftsmen, for Russian builders, being accustomed to working with timber, were not yet skilled in the stone-mason's craft. Moreover it was from Byzantium that Christianity had come to Russia; and it was right, therefore, that the Greeks should teach the newly converted pagans what kind of dwelling was appropriate for the God of the Christians. A rectangular plan, semi-circular or polygonal apses projecting at the eastern end behind the altar, and domes supported on internal piers: this was the pattern of the Byzantine Orthodox church, and it was followed in the Desyatinnaya. But even in this first stone-built church, erected though it was by Greek craftsmen, the influence of Russian taste made itself felt. The church had no fewer than twenty-five domes, a number unheard of in Byzantine architecture. This multiplicity of domes was characteristic of Russian timber churches: the Cathedral of St Sophia in Novgorod *(Plate p. 22)*, for example, built as early as the 10th century—as we learn from the chronicler—had thirteen domes.

When the church was completed in 996, seven years after work had started, Vladimir was so delighted with it that he granted the tenth part of his revenues for its maintenance; and so this church, dedicated to the Dormition of the Virgin, became known as the Desyatinnaya, the Church of the Tithe.

This splendid church, built in the heyday of the Kievan kingdom, did not survive its fall. When the hordes of the Mongol khan Baty or Batu burst into the city in 1240 such of the Kievan forces as survived the battle took refuge in the Desyatinnaya along with a large number of townsfolk. In an attempt to escape they set to digging a tunnel under the church; but the building was unable to withstand the Mongol attacks and collapsed in ruin, burying the defenders under the rubble.

Other buildings dating from Vladimir's reign have likewise failed to survive the centuries. There is more to show for the reign of his successor Yaroslav the Wise, who went in for building in stone, for both military and religious purposes, on a larger scale than his father. Of the churches he built, the largest and most important—not only in Kiev itself but in the whole of Kievan Russia—was the Cathedral of St Sophia (1037 to the middle forties of the 11th century) *(Plates pp. 25-28, 31)*.

As we see it today St Sophia is not particularly impressive, for the additions and reconstructions of the 17th to 19th centuries have transformed the original building beyond recognition. Contemporaries compared it, however, with the splendours of Solomon's temple as described in the Old Testament. As originally built it was a huge structure of severe and noble lines, with its walls patterned in alternate bands of pink and white—for in accordance with Byzantine practice the alternate courses of stone and brick were not plastered over—and with thirteen low domes on polygonal drums. At the east end were five apses, and to the north, west and south were single-storey open arcades. On the west front were two stair-towers giving access to the gallery, which extended as far as the altar and opened into the space under the dome through handsome arches. During the service the Prince's household and court sat at the west end of the gallery, and the doors of the stair-towers were guarded by watchful sentinels, ready to bar the way against any intruder.

The interior of the cathedral was splendidly finished, with its rich mosaics on a gold ground, its frescoes, its flooring of red slate, and its gold and silver vessels gleaming in the light of the countless lamps which illuminated the church.

Most of the mosaics and frescoes have been preserved. (It may be noted that the combination of mosaics and frescoes is a specifically Russian feature: the interiors of Byzantine churches were decorated with either the one or the other but not with both). Particularly fine are the mosaics in the central apse behind the altar which, following the accepted tradition, show the Virgin in the upper part, with a representation of the Liturgical Eucharist (the Communion of the Apostles) below, and—below this again—the Fathers of the Church and other teachers of the Word. The Virgin is represented in the *Orans* pose, raising her arms in the gesture of prayer *(Plate p. 28)*. She wears a purple tunic with a white kerchief hanging at the waist and a brownish-violet cloak decorated with gold stars round the hem. This figure was popularly known as the "Virgin of the Invulnerable Wall", for the wall containing this mosaic was reputed to be the only one which had survived undamaged the destruction of Kiev by the Mongols. In the Middle Ages, therefore, this image was particularly venerated by the people of Kiev.

When you look at the mosaics in the apse from some distance away, so that the broad dark outlines of the figures are no longer visible, the whole thing seems to come suddenly to life. This effect is due largely to the technique of mosaic-working used. The smalt cubes were not laid in a single plane, as is the modern practice, but at a slight angle to one another, so that light striking the mosaics is refracted at varying angles, creating the impression of a "live", glittering surface.

The frescoes in St Sophia are not all on religious themes. In the north, west and south arcades, for example, were portraits of Yaroslav the Wise, his wife the Princess Irina and their sons and daughters

—the only portraits known in Russian monumental painting of the 11th century. These frescoes are in a poor state of preservation, and our knowledge of the general composition comes from a drawing by the 17th century Dutch artist Abraham van Westerveldt. It is still possible, however, to make out the figures of four princesses, Yaroslav's daughters, ranged one behind the other in order of seniority— which the artist also indicates by making each one slightly smaller than the one before. In front, holding candles, are Elizabeth, later Queen of Norway, and Anne, later the wife of Henry I of France; behind them is Anastasia, who was to become Queen of Hungary; and behind her again is the youngest sister, whose name is not known *(Plate p. 26)*.

Of particular interest are the paintings in the stair-towers, which are thought to have been commissioned by Yaroslav himself—for the towers were evidently connected by corridors with the Prince's own apartments. These paintings introduce us into the atmosphere of court life—the Imperial court of Byzantium and the princely court of Kiev. They show the famous Hippodrome of Constantinople with the Emperor and Empress and their court sitting in boxes watching boxers, dancers and musicians; entertainers in grotesque masks; and a great variety of animals, often shown in hunting scenes.

The paintings in the towers of St Sophia throw a ray of light on a corner of a long vanished world. We know from various sources, including lives of Russian saints and the *byliny* (folk epics), that the Princes of Kiev, like other princes, were passionately devoted to hunting and were accustomed to while away their leisure hours by watching the antics of various kinds of entertainers and listening to music and singing. The frescoes in St Sophia, however, are the only representations of these themes in the whole of Russian mediaeval painting.

At first sight it may appear strange that such purely secular themes should be represented on the walls of a church. There is no cause for surprise, however, for in the Middle Ages—as we shall have occasion to note again in the course of this book—religious and secular life were so closely bound up together that it is sometimes difficult to determine where the one begins and the other leaves off. This can be illustrated by another example. Until the 15th century there was no public building in Russian towns corresponding to the *rathaus* or town hall of western Europe, and the cathedral would serve in its place. On the upper floor of one of the towers of St Sophia in Kiev was a room in which the Prince held counsel with the boyars and administered justice; and the courtyard of the cathedral and the galleries which opened into it were frequently occupied by a noisy popular assembly, the *Veche*, which discussed matters affecting the interests of the citizenry as a whole.

The citizens of the Russian towns took special pride in their cathedrals. In describing to some stranger the beauties of their native town they would usually begin with the churches; and the Russian chroniclers sometimes identify a particular town by referring to the churches it contains—talking, for example, of "the town with such-and-such a church".

In the first half of the 11th century buildings were erected in stone in many other towns as well as Kiev. Splendid churches were now built, for example, at Chernigov, Polotsk, Pereyaslavl-Yuzhny (Pereyaslavl in the South) and Novgorod. Of these the Cathedral of the Transfiguration in Chernigov *(Plate p. 21)* was perhaps the most sumptuously adorned church in Kievan Russia after Yaroslav's

St Sophia. It was a huge building with five domes and three apses and with a severe exterior, originally finished with alternate bands of stone and brick. On the north and south sides, next the apses, were small chapels which served as princely burial vaults. At the west end, roofed with a brilliantly gilded *shatër* ("tent"), was a tall stair-tower, and opposite this was a tiny baptistery. Within the church the gallery and the vaulted aisles which supported it opened into the space under the dome through arches borne on polygonal piers and marble columns. The slate flooring was inlaid with coloured smalt. In the soft radiance of the sun and of a multitude of lamps the mosaics would glow in vivid hues, the frescoes would become a blaze of colour, and patches of gold would tremble and flicker on the costly church vessels. Recent cleaning operations have shown that the paintings in the Cathedral of the Transfiguration were of remarkable beauty, surpassing in artistic quality even the frescoes of St Sophia. *(Plate p. 20)*.

In the fifties of the 11th century, however, the princedom of Kiev entered difficult times. In 1504 Yaroslav the Wise died. Anxious to provide for all his children and remembering the unhappy experience of his own early years, he had made a will dividing his kingdom into a number of separate apanages or feudal princedoms, which were to be inherited by his five sons and his grandson. It was a fatal mistake. By this testament Yaroslav hoped to obviate any internecine strife between his heirs, but in fact he succeeded merely in stimulating the growth of dissension. No sooner was he in his grave than there began a long and bitter series of fratricidal wars, often accompanied by popular risings. The period of personal monarchy—and with it the minimum of orderly government which was possible in the Middle Ages—came to an end and was succeeded by the chaos of feudalism.

The first bone of contention was Kiev itself; for whoever held this city might count himself *primus inter pares*. It was in vain that the dying Yaroslav, having granted Kiev to his eldest son Izyaslav, urged his other children: "Obey him as you obey me." After a century and a half during which it was constantly changing hands the "Mother of Russian Cities" finally sank to the status of the chief town of a petty feudal princedom. Two events in particular had dire consequences for the sorely tried city, and from the second of these Kiev did not recover until the latter part of the 17th century. The first of these events took place in 1169, when Kiev was captured and sacked by the forces of Andrey Bogolyubsky, Prince of Vladimir; the second was in 1240, when the city fell to the attacks of Baty and his Mongol hordes.

The restless atmosphere of these troubled times, when all men, great or small, lived in fear of what the morrow might bring, scarcely venturing to hope that they would get safely through the present day, had its effect on the country's spiritual life. Calls to renounce the things of this world and retire to a life of seclusion sounded ever more insistently, and met with some response: even princes were known to take the monastic vows, rejecting the temptations of this world, which they saw as no more than a vale of sorrow and of sin. "In truth, brethren, the vanity of this world, the temptations of this world!": this was the only message that Svyatoslav Davydovich, Prince of Chernigov, thought fit to leave with his boyars when he exchanged his armour for a cassock.

Much energy was now devoted to the building of monasteries. In the second half of the 11th century four large monasteries were built in Kiev alone—the Pechersky, the Dmitrievsky (or Mikhaylovsko-

Zlatoverkhy), the Vydubetsky and the Simeonovsky. The defences of the monasteries vied in strength with those of the castles held by princes and boyars; and in the conditions of the day this was very necessary, for often enough the monks were compelled by wars between feudal lords or by popular risings to abandon their prayer-books and buckle on their swords.

The important part played by the monasteries of western Europe in the cultural life of the Middle Ages is well known; and the same was true of Russia. During the wars between the petty feudal princedoms it was the monasteries which preserved the heritage of national culture and art. Safe within these massive walls, skilled craftsmen, artist carvers and icon-painters continued with their work; and in the seclusion of the monastic cells ancient manuscripts were transcribed and illuminated by the miniature-painters, while the impartial chroniclers, patiently recording the events of the passing day, bent over their never-ending task.

The most famous of these monastic houses in this period was the Pecherskaya Lavra[1] in Kiev, the Monastery of the Caves, which was established by two devout hermits, Anthony and Theodosius. The real founder, however, was Anthony, who in his quest for seclusion had installed himself in a cave hollowed out of the precipitous and densely wooded banks of the Dnieper. Within a short space of time other caves began to appear, for many men yearned after a life of seclusion — and a life which also offered a refuge from the oppressions of those in authority. Finally a monastery was built above ground as well. The caves were also used as burial chambers: here, for example, were buried the first Russian chronicler, Nestor (Nestor the Scribe, as he is called on the tablet which now hangs over the shrine containing his relics) and the first Russian artist mentioned in the chronicles, Alimpy, whose name is traditionally associated with the painting of the Cathedral of the Dormition in the Lavra. Popular tradition, however, also asserted that the caves contained the remains of the valiant bogatyr of the Russian epic tales, Ilya Muromets. The people of Kiev would tell visiting strangers how his body lay under a golden pall, "no taller than other men but with a spear driven through his left hand."

The principal church in the Pecherskaya Lavra was the Cathedral of the Dormition, built 1073-1078 (destroyed by enemy action during the second world war). It differend from the large town cathedrals of the period in having no stair-tower, its place at the north-west corner being taken by a small baptistery. Access to the gallery was by means of a wooden staircase built between the baptistery and the wall of the cathedral.

These features were certainly innovations, but they can be seen, in one form or another, in other buildings of the same period. The amount of building work was now increasing as it became more widely diffused throughout the population, until eventually even villages began to have stone-built churches. Thus at the end of the 11th century the Church of the Saviour *(Plate p. 16)* was built in the village of Berëstovo by Vladimir Monomakh, grandson of Yaroslav the Wise. The name of the village (from the Russian word for "birch-bark") is explained by the very ancient legend that the church was built in the birch grove in which Vladimir, "Bright Sun", had once had his dwelling. This church was built entirely in brick—the first of the kind. It has three porches, with an internal staircase leading up into the gallery from the narthex; opposite the staircase is a princely burial vault. A band of ornament resembling the classical meander runs round the top of the external walls.

Even these two examples—and many more could be quoted—are sufficient to demonstrate quite clearly that the experience of building in stone which Russian architects had acquired in the course of the preceding hundred and fifty years had pointed the way towards further creative achievements. Russian building in stone had now broken free from the artistic and other canons of Byzantium and was developing independently.

The type of decoration employed in the churches also changed. Mosaic was used for the last time in the altar of the cathedral in the Mikhaylovsko-Zlatoverkhy Monastery (St Michael with the Golden Roof) in Kiev: thereafter it was replaced by the less expensive and less laborious technique of fresco.

There can be no doubt that numerous icon-painters were at work in Kiev, the capital city of the earliest Russian kingdom. We know the name of Alimpy, who is still referred to in the 13th century as one of "surpassing skill in the painting of icons". Excavation in Kiev has brought to light the remains of an icon-painter's studio, burned down when the Mongols set fire to the city. But not a single icon which can be reliably ascribed to the Kievan school has survived: evidently their whole output was swept away by the Tatar invasion.

Some miniatures painted in books have, however, come down to us; and to some extent at least these replace the missing icons and illuminate certain other aspects of the painting of the 11th and 12th centuries.

The term "miniature" comes from the Latin *minium*, the red colouring matter—cinnabar or red lead—which the old calligraphers used in manuscripts for initial letters and rubrics. The art of miniature painting was known in Russia as early as the first half of the 11th century through the work of Byzantine and Balkan (mainly Bulgarian) artists. At first these foreign models were slavishly copied, but soon a distinct Russian school began to grow up. No doubt we can see one of the causes of its rapid development in the extraordinarily high regard felt in Kievan Russia for books and the "surpassing treasures of wisdom" they contained.

Prince Vladimir sought to establish in Kiev something equivalent to elementary schools, giving orders that "the children of nobles, the middle orders and the needy should be taken and assigned to priests and deacons in divers churches so that they might receive instruction in book learning." Yaroslav the Wise did the same at Novgorod, bringing together in the Cathedral of St Sophia a library which was of outstanding quality by the standards of the day. "Great is our profit from book learning!" cries a contemporary. "From the writings contained in books we gain wisdom and continence. These are the rivers that water the earth; these are the springs of true wisdom."

The books of this period were meticulously and beautifully produced. As in western Europe, they were written by hand on parchment. The text pages were often considerable works of graphic art in their own right, in virtue of the delicacy and beauty of the lettering. This is particularly true of the initial letters, painted in bright colours and often gilded, which were formed from an intricate pattern of scrolls and flourishes interwoven with representations of animals, human heads and other figures.

Colouring and gilding were also used in the magnificent headpieces and tailpieces and in the miniatures which were scattered through the book, their themes varying according to the subject-matter of the text. The colouring used was gouache, which took well on parchment, producing a dense velvety surface. For the groundwork gold leaf, in sheets no thicker than cigarette paper, was used, the leaf being glued to the parchment and then cut round the outline of the design —a costly technique which by the 15th century had been superseded by the use of gold paint. As can be seen, therefore, the methods of book production and of miniature painting were the same as those in use in western Europe at this period.

The oldest and most celebrated examples of the book production of Kievan Russia are the "Ostromir Gospel" (1056; in the Saltykov-Shchedrin Library in Leningrad) and the "Compendium of Svyatoslav" (1073; in the Historical Museum in Moscow). The former was produced by a certain Deacon Gregory for Ostromir, *posadnik* (mayor) of Novgorod, and was illustrated by an unknown miniature-painter with full-page portraits of the Evangelists *(Plate p. 19)*—following a practice inherited from ancient times of putting the portrait of the author at the beginning of his text. The "Compendium" was made for Prince Izyaslav, son of Yaroslav the Wise, but when Kiev was captured by his brother Svyatoslav the book acquired a new owner and a new title. This splendid manuscript contains four miniatures representing groups of bishops — the authors of the articles included in the collection. Round each group of prelates is an ornamental frame, splendidly gilded, like a schematic representation of a three-domed church, with the figure of a peacock on either side. The peacock, which in antiquity was the constant attendant of Hera-Juno, the goddess of the domestic hearth, came in early Christian and later in mediaeval art to symbolise the Christian church; for it was firmly believed that the peacock's body was incorruptible.

With their bright colouring, their use of gold, and the extraordinary delicacy of their workmanship, the miniatures put us in mind of the jeweller's craft; and in fact the jewellery of this period was of great beauty and was produced in great quantity. Gold and silver rings, bracelets and *kolty* (pendants which hung from women's headdresses over the temples) were richly set with pearls and precious stones; or they might be covered with a lace-like tracery of filigree work or with an intricate pattern of microscopic gold and silver balls, in the technique known as granulation; or they might be richly coated with niello or enamel (a vitreous compound coloured by an admixture of metal oxides).

One of the chief glories of the Kievan artists was their cloisonné enamel work, of a quality scarcely inferior to that produced in Byzantium. It was an intricate technique: on the object to be decorated the design was first scratched out, and the metal within the outline was removed; thin strips of metal were then soldered on to the ground, following the lines of the design, and the spaces between the strips were filled with enamel paste; and the object was then fired, polished after cooling, fired again, and finally burnished. This produced a delicate pattern of colour, an interplay of many hues within which glittered the golden web of the metal framework. The designs covered a wide range, from vegetable ornament to human figures, animals and birds. Perhaps the commonest theme is the bird of ill omen, Sirin—a bird with the head of a beautiful girl, evidently closely related to the sirens of classical Greece, with whose mythology and imagery Kiev was acquainted, not only through Byzantium but through contact with the art of the Greek cities on the Black Sea.

Of equal quality is the niello work, particularly on gold objects. Niello is a compound of various metals and metalloids, most commonly of tin, lead, silver and sulphur. The constituent elements were melted separately and then fused together; and the mixture was then melted again, allowed to cool, and pounded into a fine powder. At this point the alchemist was transformed into an artist. He took the object to be decorated, which had been got ready for the purpose, cut out the design, sprinkled it with the niello powder and then with borax, and put the whole thing in a kiln on a low fire. Using a wire with a flattened end, he spread out the niello evenly over the appropriate parts of the design during firing. Then, after the final firing, the article was polished and burnished in the same way as the enamel jewellery.

The precious metals were also used for making a variety of articles for both religious and secular use—the bindings of liturgical books, communion vessels, lustres, candlesticks, lavers, wine cups, spoons, and so on. If at a feast given by a prince or a boyar the food and drink were served in anything other than gold or silver vessels this was regarded as a slight on the guests. The warriors of Prince Vladimir's retinue, having been invited by their master to a feast, were gravely offended to find the table set with wooden spoons; whereupon Vladimir, recognising his error, had perforce to acquire silver ones in their place.

The *bogatyrs* of this period also drank their wine from huge aurochs horns set in gold and silver. Two such horns bound with silver were found during the excavation of the "Black Tomb", a funeral *kurgan* erected over the remains of some unknown 10th century warrior not far from Chernigov. On the binding of one of these (now in the Historical Museum in Moscow) is a decoration—partly embossed and partly engraved, with some niello work added—consisting of representations in relief of scaly monsters with intertwined tails, dogs attacking the monsters, a bird wearing a crown, and small running figures of a man and a woman. The man is turning round as he runs to shoot at the bird with his bow.

The bird is evidently, however, no ordinary fowl, for the arrows are rebounding from its body and turning back against the archer *(Plate p. 14)*. It is supposed that the decoration on this horn represents episodes from the *bylina* of Ivan Godinovich. This *bogatyr* won as his wife the Princess Nastasya of Chernigov, who was already the promised bride of Kashchey the Deathless; whereupon Kashchey set out in pursuit, overcame his rival and bound him in chains. Then the birds of ill omen appeared from nowhere, foretelling the doom of the crafty victor. Kashchey the Deathless fired arrow after arrow at them; but in vain, for Ivan Godinovich cast a spell on the arrows so that they returned against the evildoer who had fired them.

The belief in marvels and magic spells prevailed throughout the whole of the Middle Ages, and we need hardly be surprised to find it so active in Kievan Russia. The men of the mediaeval period had their share of very real misfortunes, but in addition they were haunted at every turn, at every step they took, by a host of imaginary terrors. They had only to hear a board creaking in their house, the croak of a raven or the barking of a dog, to cross the path of a monk, to have a bad dream, and at once they wondered what evil these omens might portend. In their fear of the unknown these things often seemed to them more terrifying than war or famine or pestilence, and they sought protection against the forces of evil in the intercession of the saints or—even more readily—in the well-tried remedies of pagan antiquity, the use of amulets and talismans, of magic spells and incantations. A whole century has passed since the conversion of Russia, complains the Metropolitan John, but the ordinary people are still surreptitiously offering sacrifices to Chernobog, the Black God, to the well-spirit and to the water-sprite. With the experience of so many subsequent centuries to go on, however, we know that traces of pagan superstitions survived much longer than the worthy Metropolitan could suspect. For did not peasants living in villages in the Dnieper area in the 19th century still put a nettle plant on the threshold of their houses during what was called Rusala's Week in order to protect themselves from the sly tricks of the water nymphs? And did not the peasants go in search of a flowering fern on Midsummer's Eve? And was there not also the ill-omened Bare Mountain on which, according to a belief long cherished in Kiev, the witches gathered at night to hold their revels, trampling down the grass so that the mountain top became bald and bare? Traditions of this kind were found everywhere, but were particularly common in Kiev—no doubt because in times of remote antiquity this had been one of the great centres of Slav paganism.

All this now belongs to the distant past, and the Kievan kingdom has long vanished from the face of the earth. Its memory still lives, however, in the pages of the chronicles, in the *byliny* and folk tales, in the luminous frescoes of St Sophia, and in the bright colours of the Kievan enamels and miniatures.

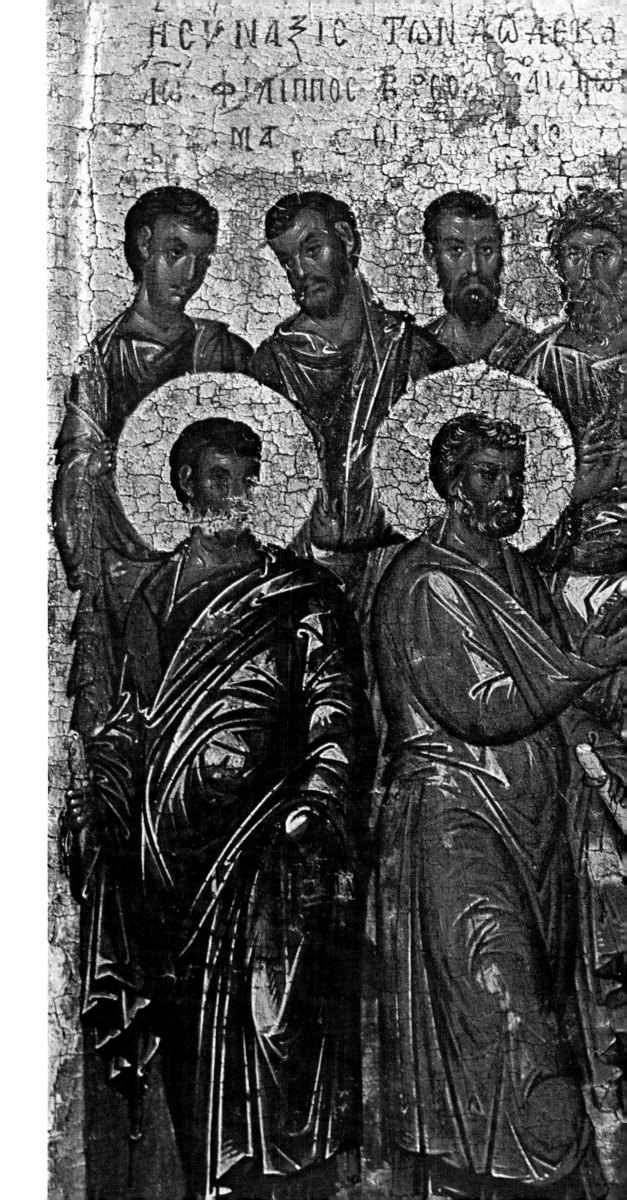

38

III "NO CITY MIGHTIER THAN VLADIMIR, NO RULER MIGHTIER THAN HER PRINCE"

The splitting up of the Kievan kingdom into a number of independent apanages or feudal princedoms led to the development of local schools of art—the schools of Novgorod, Kiev, Vladimir-Suzdal, Galicio-Volhynia, and so on. There were many of these local schools—indeed one for each of the newly established political units from which they take their names. At first the works produced by the various schools—particularly in the field of painting—showed no very significant differences; but as time went on the artistic ideals of Byzantium receded into the background and local preferences and distinctive local identities began to assert themselves ever more strongly. The architecture of the princedom of Vladimir-Suzdal in the 12th century, for example, is so individual that it can be distinguished at once from the architecture of Chernigov, Novgorod, Smolensk or other Russian towns; and among the monuments of the pre-Mongol period the churches of Vladimir-Suzdal stand out as the most beautiful and most magnificent. This splendour is found not only in their interiors, which have the same sumptuousness as St Sophia in Kiev or the Cathedral of the Saviour in Chernigov, but extends also to their external architecture, which is of princely magnificence. The reason for this is clear: in the 12th century, with the decline of the Princedom of Kiev, there was developing in north-eastern Russia a second Russian kingdom with its capital at Vladimir.

The rise of Vladimir began at the end of the 11th century, when the area fell by right of inheritance to Vladimir Monomakh. Having thereupon come into conflict with Prince Oleg of Chernigov, Vladimir felt the need of a secure fortress—for he could have little reliance on the old-established towns in this area, Rostov and Suzdal. Accordingly, on the high bank of the River Klyazma, on the hills which commanded the road from Ryazan and Murom, he caused a ring of earthen ramparts to be constructed, surmounted by stout oak palisades and surrounded by deep ditches which linked the ends of natural ravines. Within these defences were the Prince's *terem* (tower or keep) and the residences of his boyars, along with various store-rooms and domestic offices; and, as was proper, there soared above these secular buildings the radiant golden dome of the Church of the Saviour, the first stone church to be built in this area. And so there came into being the town of Vladimir, baptised by its founder with his own name.

Vladimir's son Yury, known as Dolgoruky ("Long Arms"), established his capital in the old city of Suzdal and showed little interest in his father's creation. Nor indeed did he spend much time in this or any other city, for his whole life was spent in expeditions to the south, dreaming of the throne of the Kievan kingdom, until at last he died ingloriously by drinking poisoned wine at the very moment when his object seemed to have been achieved. Two buildings dating from the time of Yury Dolgoruky have survived in north-eastern Russia—the Cathedral of the Saviour in Pereyaslavl-Zalessky, a severe

structure with massive walls and a single dome, and the Church of SS. Boris and Gleb in the princely village of Kideksha, now almost unrecognisable under the reconstructions carried out in later periods.

The golden age of the princedom of Vladimir-Suzdal and of its art came in the reigns of Yury's sons, Andrey (1157-1175) and Vsevolod III (1177-1212). The latter was the father of a large family, which earned him the name of "Big Brood".

Having taken part in many of his father's campaigns against Kiev, Prince Andrey realised clearly the fruitlessness of Yury's aspirations. His own ambitions lay elsewhere: his dream was to establish in north-eastern Russia a powerful new kingdom with Vladimir as its capital. His choice of Vladimir was no accident: he saw the advantages of its convenient situation, the surroun-

ding forests which served as a defence and also provided a supply of building material, and the abundance of water, so essential in the event of a long siege and so favourable to the development of trade. The nearby Volga played the same part in the economy of this area as the Dnieper in the areas to the south. Finally there was one other important factor in the choice of Vladimir. The population of the town consisted mainly of craftsmen, small traders and peasants, who were in feudal vassalage to the boyars of Rostov; and it was in these classes that Andrey hoped to find support against the old noble families of Rostov and Suzdal, among whom his ambitious plans had provoked a storm of protest.

An alliance between Prince and townsfolk was a common phenomenon in the feudal world, and was usually successful, at least for a period. At any rate Andrey's political calculations turned out to be correct: the boyars' resistance was broken, apparently for good. Now the Prince was able to devote himself to the embellishment of his new capital, which was to bear witness to the success of his plans and accordingly must outshine all the other cities of Russia.

Ceaselessly throughout the day and night, therefore, carts laden with white limestone rolled from the quarries of the lower Oka valley to the hill of Vladimir. Great numbers of craftsmen were employed —summoned, as the chronicler tells us, "from every corner of the earth". Among them were heard the abrupt accent of the north Russians, the melodious speech of the south, and even dialects from some countries of western Europe. There was nothing unusual about this, for in the Middle Ages groups of masons, painters and other craftsmen were accustomed to travel from place to place and from country to country, offering their services to any who stood in need of them.

Under Andrey's impulsion the town of Vladimir, which in the reign of Yury Dolgoruky had been scarcely more than a huddle of mean houses, changed beyond recognition in the short space of some seven or eight years. By the year 1165 the lower slopes of the hill of Vladimir were resounding with the constant noise and bustle of the traders' and craftsmen's quarter. Vladimir Monomakh's cave town on the hill was ringed with new fortifications, and in its southern corner rose a church of outstanding beauty, the Cathedral of the Dormition. Its walls, dazzlingly white in the sun, and its helm-shaped golden dome with the cross standing out against the sky were visible for a distance of many miles. Beside the old town of Vladimir Monomakh stood the "New Town" with its two churches—which themselves were not new—and the newly built mansions of the Prince and his favourites. It was entered by four gateways. The principal entrance, which was on the west side, as in Kiev, was called the Golden Gate (no doubt because the massive oak doors were bound with gilded bronze). Above the entrance stood the Church of the Laying On of the Virgin's Veil. In front of the Golden Gate the townsfolk swore allegiance to their Prince, and also greeted the visitors from distant places who were always welcome to the city. The Volga Gate on the south side of the town gave access to the landing-place on the River Klyazma, where vessels belonging to Vladimir and to other cities on distant shores, laden with cargoes of goods, swayed gently by the wharf amid the creaking of anchor chains.

Of all these structures—the walls, the palaces and the churches—nothing remains today but the Golden Gate and the Cathedral of the Dormition. Of the original gateway, indeed, only the main arch is left: all the rest of the present structure dates from the 18th century. Nor is the Cathedral as we see it today the original structure; but its rebuilding took place in the same century in which it was built, between 1185 and 1189. It still stands today as it stood then—a massive building with five domes, majestic splayed doorways, and narrow slits of windows in deep embrasures which are also framed in a series of receding arches. Half way up the walls is a band of blind arcades, and there are similar arcades round the top of the apse walls. Above the windows are occasional sculptured mascarons *(Plate p. 42)*. The original cathedral built by Prince Andrey was of rather smaller dimensions, with a single dome and two towers with gilded tent roofs on the west front; but it, too, had bands of blind arcades, the spaces between the colonnettes being decorated with painted figures of peacocks and saints. In the reconstruction and enlargement of the cathedral in 1185-1189 arched openings were made in these walls, which were now inside the walls of the new building. Only a few fragments of the 12th century paintings in the Cathedral have been preserved; the rest of the paintings now visible were done in the early years of the 15th century, when the artists included the famous Andrey Rublëv.

On 28th August, the feast of the Dormition of the Mother of God, enormous numbers of people flocked to Vladimir from all over Russia. Two cords were drawn through the crowd, beginning inside the church and stretching across the Cathedral Square to the Bishop's Palace, and on these cords were hung gold-brocaded ecclesiastical vestments, richly adorned with pearls and precious stones. The immense crowd gazed with bated breath as these splendid fabrics fluttered in the breeze, in a shimmer of gold and an interplay of vivid hues. Then between these gorgeous walls, which seemed almost alive in their rich colouring and constant movement, an endless queue of people—subdued and silent, almost overwhelmed by the luxury which surrounded them—made their way into the church. The fame of this splendid cathedral, and of the fabulous wealth of the northern ruler who had built it, spread far and wide, multiplied a hundredfold by popular report.

Why, it may be asked, did these pious pilgrims flock to Vladimir on the feast of the Dormition?

Having demonstrated by force of arms the superiority of his new northern capital to the older capital in the south, Prince Andrey was concerned to make Vladimir a centre not only of the political but also of the spiritual life of the country. This position had previously been occupied by Kiev, at least in religious matters; for Kiev contained the residence of the Metropolitan, the famous Pechersky Monastery with the caves in which the earliest holy men of Kiev were buried, and many churches in which were treasured some of the most ancient and most revered objects of worship in Russia. In his concern to cast off the spiritual suzerainty of Kiev, and by the same token to free himself from that of Byzantium, Andrey himself appointed the Bishop of Vladimir—though hitherto all bishops had had to be confirmed by the Metropolitan of Kiev—and established the cult of local miracle-workers. In addition he brought from Kiev the famous icon of the Mother of God, the Virgin of Vladimir which was one of the most hallowed objects of mediaeval Russia and is now in the Tretyakov Gallery *(Plate p. 40)*.

The Virgin of Vladimir is represented in the pose known as "Our Lady's Tenderness". She is shown at half length, her head bent over the infant whom she holds in her right arm. The compressed lips, the hint of a frown, the expression of profound anguish in her dark eyes create an extraordinarily expressive image of a mother oppressed by the foreboding of evil to come. The child presses his cheek

50

to her face; one of his arms is round her neck, the other clutches her stole. In this convulsive movement and in the upturned glance with which he seeks his mother's eye we divine a momentary impulse of fright and an unspoken plea for help. The unknown Byzantine master of the late 11th or early 12th century has expressed in this icon, with tremendous force, the whole profundity of wordless human suffering. The Virgin's face is painted with outstanding skill. The pink colouring of her cheeks seems to flow from within the dark golden brown of her skin. The translucent olive shadows give tenderness to the lines of the face and, clustering more thickly under the eyes, strengthen the expression of tragic sorrow. The only highlight is provided by a touch of scarlet on the lips. The infant's face is painted in brighter colours and the shadows are even more translucent—no doubt in an attempt to convey the particular colouring of childhood.

It was probably this perfection of artistry that gave rise to the legend that the icon was the work of St Luke himself, the patron saint of painters. Moreover it had the reputation throughout Russia of being a wonder-working icon, and pilgrims oppressed by the troubles and sorrows of this world came from far and wide to worship it. Thus when this widely revered icon was set up in the Cathedral of the Dormition the Mother of God became the patron of the city of Vladimir and of the Princes of Vladimir, sanctifying all their actions with the prestige of her name, and the icon itself became known as the "Virgin of Vladimir".

Andrey built two other churches in honour of his heavenly patron. The first of these is the Church of the Protection of the Virgin on the River Nerl, the leading building in the monastery of the same name which then occupied the site *(Plate p. 52)*.

The feast of the Protection of the Virgin is a purely Russian celebration which was introduced at this period. The legend of the Protection (i.e., the Virgin's veil) is of Byzantine origin. The story goes that the blessed Andrey Yurodivy (Andrew the Simple), while praying with a disciple in the famous Church of the Blachernae, saw the Mother of God standing in the principal doorway of the church. Unseen to any others, she went up to the altar and spread her veil over the worshippers, as if promising her intercession in any sorrow or misfortune. The Mother of God was represented in this pose in the icons of the Protection of the Virgin which from the 14th century onwards appeared throughout Russia in increasing numbers. The first church built in honour of the Protection of the Virgin was the one on the Nerl (1165).

The site selected for the monastery was subject to flooding by the Klyazma and the Nerl in spring; and to meet this difficulty the builders first erected an artificial mound, facing it with fair white stone and providing channels for rainwater to run off, and only then began the construction of their church.

The mound is now covered by many centuries' deposit of soil, burying its stone facing and changing its shape. Nothing is now visible of the monastic buildings, or of the splendid stone arcade which once surrounded the church. But the church itself still stands as it has stood for eight centuries, gracefully mirrored in the waters of the River Nerl, which is now much silted up. This is undoubtedly the most beautiful and most graceful of the old Russian churches. It is quite small, with a single dome and narrow apses projecting only a short distance from the nave. The soaring upward movement and the

delicate and harmonious lines are accentuated by the slender pilasters which give proportion to the walls, the tall narrow windows, and the blind arcades with rather elongated colonnettes which run round the building. The effect is still further enhanced by the beautiful splayed doorways richly decorated with carving, the sculptured mascarons, and the griffins and figures of Biblical characters above the windows and in the *zakomary* (the rounded gable heads).

The year 1165, in which the Church of the Protection was finished, also saw the completion of the nearby palace of Bogolyubovo. The name indicates that this was the dwelling-place of God-fearing people; but the actual story of Bogolyubovo has little enough connection with God. The boyars of Rostov and Suzdal, who had resisted the absolutist policy of the Grand Prince, had been forced into outward compliance but had by no means lost hope of securing their revenge; and since a rebellion of the great feudal lords might flare up whenever a favourable opportunity occurred it was essential to maintain a vigilant watch on Rostov and Suzdal. The Prince therefore needed a powerful fortress on the road between Suzdal and Vladimir which should serve as a constantly manned strong point and watching post. In order that the building might be completed without delay or hindrance Andrey sought the help of his heavenly patroness. In the "Account of the Wonders Wrought by the Icon of Our Lady of Vladimir" we are told, among other marvels, that when the icon was brought from Kiev the horses halted at the exact place where the Prince had in mind to build his fortress, and could not be persuaded to move from the spot. This "wonder" was, of course, interpreted as meaning that the Mother of God desired that a church should be built in her honour on this site. Where a church was to be built it was reasonable to build a palace; and in those days a palace must necessarily be fortified. And so the palace of Bogolyubovo was built, and Prince Andrey became known as Bogolyubsky, the man who loved God.

All that now remains of the great complex of 12th century buildings—the palace itself, the Church of the Nativity of Our Lady, and various domestic and military structures—is the lower part of the north tower, handsomely built in stone, the passage leading from the tower into the gallery of the church, and part of the adjacent north wall of the church. The rest of the structure dates from the 17th to 19th centuries. Fragments which have survived show that the palaces of the princedom of Vladimir-Suzdal presented the same architectural features as the churches of this area, including the use of stone and the decoration of the external walls with blind arcades.

After Andrey Bogolyubsky's death in 1175—tradition had it that he was killed in the north tower of his palace, the one still visible today—all that he had achieved seemed doomed to destruction. His death led to a rising of the people of Bogolyubovo and the citizens of Vladimir, who were devoted to his cause; and when this had been quelled the quarrels of the feudal lords flared up once again. This continued for two years until Andrey's brother Vsevolod, "Big Brood", became Grand Prince and, after carrying out savage reprisals, set about restoring order in all the apanages of the princedom. He had the advantage of a well-trained army, so numerous that —in the picturesque language of the "Lay of Igor's Raid"—the Prince's warriors might have emptied the Don with their helmets and spilled the Volga with their oars; and he also pursued a successful foreign policy, achieved military victory, and maintained wide-ranging trading and cultural relations with the countries of the West and with Byzantium. In short, the twenty-five years of Vsevolod's reign were the most brilliant period in the history of the princedom of Vladimir. Throughout these years much building was done, and a local chronicler records that, unlike Andrey, Vsevolod no longer found it necessary to "look to the *nemtsy* (Germans)[2] for his craftsmen." Among the buildings now erected were a number of monasteries and churches and the Prince's palace in Vladimir. The only part of the palace which survives is the Cathedral of St Dmitry (Demetrius), which—like the church in Bogolyubovo— seems to have been directly connected with the palace.

At first glance the Cathedral of St Dmitry *(Plate p. 46)*, built between 1193 and 1197, resembles the churches of Andrey Bogolyubsky's reign. Like them, it was single-domed, with a vaulted roof, the same articulation of the external walls and the same splayed doorways, slit-like windows and blind arcades. Sculptured decoration, however, which was only sparingly employed in Andrey's buildings, now develops into a riot of ornament. An interwoven pattern of leaves and ribbons fills the spaces between the windows in the drum under the dome, and extends to the arches, the cornices, and the colonnettes and capitals of the blind arcades. The whole of the upper part of the walls is covered with carved representations of a multitude of fabulous creatures, stylised plants, galloping horsemen and saints; and other figures of saints are fitted in between the colonnettes of the blind arcades.

Apart from some scenes with an identifiable content—Vsevolod with a child in his lap and his sons kneeling in front of him, the Baptism of Christ, the Ascension of Alexander, and one or two others—the significance of these reliefs presents us with a puzzle which scholars have been unable to solve: none of the suggestions put forward so far seems plausible. Perhaps, however, there is no point in seeking to interpret them: their main interest lies elsewhere. For surely these sirens and hippogriffs, these lions with human faces and tails in the form of vegetable tendrils, and all the other fantastic images conceived by the fertile imagination of the ancient pagans are quite out of place on the walls of a Christian church? Their appearance in Vladimir, however, is not fortuitous. In this area Christianity was introduced later than in the territory of Kiev, and had difficulty in establishing itself. Even in the early 12th century there were many who remained faithful to the ancient gods. Luxuriant patterns of pagan ornament were woven into the fabric of the Christian legends, and vestiges of pagan conceptions can frequently be detected in Christian art. If we remember that the Cathedral of St Dmitry was built and decorated by local craftsmen we need not be surprised by the type of ornament they preferred; nor is it surprising that the Church authorities were displeased. In public no one dared to run counter to the "ambitious Prince of Vladimir", as he was called; but the Bishop's chronicler, enumerating all the buildings erected by Vsevolod, made no mention of the

most grandiose and magnificent of them all, treating the Cathedral of St Dmitry as if it had vanished from the face of the earth.

The cathedral contains fragments of a 12th century painting of the Last Judgment *(Plate p. 47)*, showing St Peter leading a procession of the righteous into Paradise, in which we see the Mother of God, the patriarchs Abraham, Isaac and Jacob, and the twelve Apostles seated on golden thrones, with angels behind them. Some parts of the painting are very fine, others are of poorer quality. Clearly a number of different hands are at work; and we know from other sources that on large commissions many different craftsmen were employed.

The Cathedral of St Dmitry was the last great achievement of the architecture of Vladimir. Building work continued until Vsevolod's death in 1212, under the impulsion of the Prince himself, the Princess his wife, and John, Bishop of Vladimir; but the character of the architecture changed. It became less exuberant, more austere; brick was used as well as stone, and the sculptured ornament disappeared from the walls of the churches.

After Vsevolod's death the bloody rivalries between the feudal lords were renewed. The unified Russian state, created at the cost of so much effort, began to break up into fragments. Vladimir ceased to be the capital, and its artistic life gradually died out as its craftsmen went off to other feudal centres in quest of employment. There was no shortage of work in these other towns, but the development of their art followed a rather different pattern from that of Vladimir. And of course time was moving on: it was now the second quarter of the 13th century, and tastes were showing a distinct change.

Of these later buildings, perhaps the closest in style to the 12th century churches in Vladimir are the Cathedral of the Nativity of the Virgin in Suzdal and the Cathedral of St George in Yuryev-Polsky[3].

The Cathedral of the Nativity *(Plate p. 54)* was originally built by Vladimir Monomakh at the turn of the 11th and 12th centuries. The use of brick indicates that it was the work of craftsmen from Kiev, no doubt brought by Vladimir when he came to take over his princedom. Between 1222 and 1225 it was thought necessary for some reason—perhaps because the exterior of the original church was too plain for contemporary taste—to reconstruct it. The brick walls were torn down and rebuilt in tufa, and the architectural details—the slender pilasters which articulate the external walls, the carved doorways, the colonnettes on the apses and the blind arcades—were also of stone. The decorative effect was achieved by the contrast between the finely dressed stone detailing and the irregular porous texture of the grey stone in which the walls were built, so that the details stand out sharply against the darker background.

The present church is very different from its 13th century appearance. Like most old buildings, it was frequently rebuilt and added to in later centuries. In the 1950s and early 1960s a number of later additions in brick were cleared away; but the only part of the 13th century building which still survives is the lower part of the walls, including the blind arcades.

The church contains some remains of ancient paintings (1233). In the upper part of the southern apse, for example, are the figure of two saintly old men with the austere and emaciated faces of ascetics

(Plate p. 55). Most of the painting, however, consists of geometric and vegetable ornament. A stylised pattern of intertwining plants also decorates the walls of the niches under the gallery, in the burial vault of the Princes and Bishops of Suzdal.

Other features from the same period which have survived are the double doors in the west and south doorways. These are clad with bronze and decorated with engravings of Biblical scenes and various saints, intricately damascened in gold.

The Cathedral of the Nativity was rebuilt by Prince George, son of Vsevolod "Big Brood", with whom the reader is already acquainted. The Cathedral of St George in Yuryev-Polsky *(Plate p. 58)*, however, is associated with another of Vsevolod's sons, Svyatoslav.

Yuryev-Polsky, then the principal city of Svyatoslav's apanage, had since 1152 possessed a small and modest church dedicated to St George the Victorious. The builders of this church seem to have been poor workmen, or perhaps they were working with poor material: at any rate the church soon began to show signs of dilapidation, and by the third decade of the following century stood in urgent need of repair. But Svyatoslav would not hear of repairing the unassuming old building, which seemed an affront to his dignity as a Prince. In 1230, therefore, the church was demolished, and within three years there arose in its place a fine new church built entirely of fair white stone, like the churches of Vladimir. But none of the churches in Vladimir—not even St Dmitry—was so lavishly adorned with carved ornament. The carvings covered the whole surface of the walls and doorways, from the ground upwards, as if the craftsmen who built the church were afraid of leaving any corner without ornament. And what a variety of subject matter is represented in these carvings! From the blind arcades the stone images of saints look down with unseeing eyes, and the walls, colonnettes and doorway arches are covered with a riot of vegetable ornament, enfolding in its coils a variety of human figures and animals and birds. The eye can scarcely follow the endlessly changing pattern; nor is it easy to distinguish in this confusion of themes any over-all scheme of decoration or any controlling idea behind the profusion of ornament. This is because the Cathedral of St George as it now exists belongs to two different periods, the 13th and the 15th centuries. In the 15th century the roof of the church collapsed, carrying with it the upper part of the walls, and in 1471 the Grand Prince of Moscow, Ivan III, sent the famous Moscow builder and sculptor, Vasily Ermolin, to repair it. It cannot be said, however, that the rebuilding of St George's was one of his most successful achievements. The walls as he rebuilt them were too low, so that the band of blind arcades came almost immediately under the roof and the building as a whole was of rather squat and clumsy proportions. Moreover Ermolin had apparently neither the time nor the patience to work out the pattern of the original carved ornament, and in many cases the arrangement of the stones was determined largely by their size. The result was like a child's jigsaw in which all the pieces were fitted into place but the pattern was lost.

Like other early Russian churches, the cathedrals of Vladimir-Suzdal were originally decorated with paintings; but unfortunately only a few of them have preserved any of these paintings, and then only in the form of fragments. We are still worse off in relation to the icons of this period. We have a small group of icons which are attributed to the Vladimir-Suzdal (or Rostov-Suzdal) school *(Plate*

p. 56), partly on account of their provenance, partly on the basis of stylistic comparison with, for example, the frescoes in St Dmitry. The trouble is that the icons of the 12th and early 13th centuries, no matter from what part of Russia they come, mostly express the general style of the period, and it is a matter of extreme difficulty to identify distinctive local features. The only icon which we can say with confidence was painted in Vladimir, and nowhere else, is the Virgin of Bogolyubovo; but this icon is in such a state of ruin that it cannot be used as a basis of stylistic comparison.

The situation is very different with the art of the silversmith and the goldsmith, where we find distinct differences in local styles. These crafts were no less developed in this area than in the territory of Kiev. The princes and boyars wore garments decorated with patterned gold and silver plaques, garnished with coloured silks, brocaded with metal threads and set with pearls and precious stones. Their wives wore headdresses from which hung strings of jingling pendants, and costly rings glittering in all the colours of the rainbow. The warriors' armour and weapons were adorned with gold and silver, and at their feasts food and drink were served in gold and silver vessels. All this was part of the way of life of noble families in this period, not only in Russia but in other countries: the surprising and characteristic feature, however, is that at the sight of any of the articles produced by the local jewellers we are at once reminded of the churches of Vladimir. This is natural enough, of course, in the case of objects serving a liturgical use—for example reliquaries, tabernacles and censers, which are often in the form of churches with one or more domes—particularly in the mediaeval period but also in later centuries. But we find the same thing in objects not merely of a secular but of a frivolous nature—in articles of personal adornment, for example.

Among the commonest of such articles are *naruchi*, a kind of broad bracelet or bangle used to gather the sleeves of under garments at the wrist. They are in two halves, which are joined by long hinges, and are made of silver embossed with relief ornament, sometimes with the addition of niello but usually with a rich coating of gilt. (We may remark in passing that whereas the Kievans liked the combination of niello and enamel with gold the citizens of Vladimir preferred the use of gold on silver). Each half of the bracelet had a raised rim, either plain or ornamented, and there was sometimes also an embossed ridge running across the middle—producing something of the same effect as the cornices and pilasters which were used to break up the walls of churches. The rest of the surface is usually divided into separate panels by embossed gilt colonnettes and arches. In these golden cages are contained all manner of fierce creatures—snarling lions with birds' legs, lashing their tails in impotent fury at winged monsters which seem to have descended from the walls of St Dmitry's or St George's at the behest of some magician. Sometimes, too, there are human figures; but the commonest figure of all is the griffin. This fantastic creature, a cross between a bird and a beast of prey, had been a favourite decorative theme on gold and silver objects from time immemorial. The ancient Greeks had called the griffin the "guardian of treasure" and had used it as a decoration on the doors of the royal treasuries; and it had the same significance in the thought of the mediaeval world. It is of interest to note that these bracelets, like most of the jewellery we possess dating from the late 12th and the 13th centuries, were found in hoards or "treasures". It must be added, however, that the representations of griffins guarded the valuables entrusted to their care not by inspiring terror but by appealing to conscience—and with some success, for the famous Treasure of Vladimir lay undisturbed in the ground for six and a half centuries before being discovered in 1896 *(Plates p. 45)*.

But these fabulous creatures, so fantastically combined with human figures and even with representations of saints, are not the only reminiscence of church art and architecture; for do not these tiny

gilded arches on their silver background remind us of the gilded arcades standing out against the plain white surface of the cathedral walls? Evidently the churches of Vladimir, combining severe architectural form with a riot of carved ornament, had made a powerful impression on the contemporary imagination.

As we survey the art of Vladimir we are inevitably struck by the contrast between the magnitude of its achievement and the brief period of its flowering. For by the end of the first quarter of the 13th century the kingdom of the Grand Princes of Vladimir, lately so powerful, was weltering in blood and ravaged by interminable fratricidal wars. And while these troubles were at their height came the first intimations of a greater catastrophe. The teeming Mongol hordes from the steppes of Asia advanced on the land of Rus, leaving a wake of smoking ruins and mountains of corpses wherever they passed. In February 1238 they reached Vladimir. The citizens resisted heroically, although they realised that this was the beginning of the end: an end that was hastened by the fatal circumstance that there had not been time to rebuild the old timber west gate of the city, the Klyazma Gate, in stone. To make matters worse, the besieging army managed to break through the walls near the Church of the Saviour. The city was captured, plundered and set on fire, and the inhabitants were put to the sword. The Cathedral of the Dormition was burned down, and in the fire perished the Bishop of Vladimir and the family of George, son of Vsevolod, last Prince of Vladimir, who had taken refuge in the gallery of the church.

The princedom of Vladimir-Suzdal now disappeared from history, but the artistic traditions which had developed here were not destined to die. We shall find them renewing themselves and coming to fresh flowering in a new soil, in the architecture of Moscow under its Grand Princes,

IV LORD NOVGOROD THE GREAT AND HIS YOUNGER BROTHER PSKOV

In the history of mediaeval Russia Novgorod occupies a position of exceptional importance, and no account of the artistic culture of the period can be complete if it neglects the art of Novgorod. Conversely, the art of Novgorod cannot be fully understood without some knowledge, even in the most general terms, of certain features of the historical development of the city; for though in many ways it resembles the history of other Russian cities it also shows a number of features peculiar to itself.

The basis of Novgorod's prosperity was trade, the rapid development of which was promoted by the abundance of lakes and rivers in the area, and above all by the proximity of the sea. None of the cities of ancient Rus extended its trading relations so widely as Novgorod, which had dealings with almost the whole known world. The great water route "from the Varangians to the Greeks" passed through Novgorod, and to Novgorod came vessels from Byzantium, Sweden, Denmark and —from the 14th century onwards—the cities of the Hanseatic League. The shops of Novgorod sold not only local products but fabrics and precious objects from the East, spices and wine from distant lands; and in return the amber-yellow wax of Novgorod and splendid furs from the northern countries found a ready market in Byzantium, Italy and France.

The development of trade and of craft industry always go hand in hand. Novgorod was no exception to the rule: it was a city not only of merchants but of skilled craftsmen. There were so many of them that many streets, and even whole districts of the city, were named after the various trades; and archaeological excavation has recovered the objects they produced in stone, metal, wood or bone—furniture, dishes and utensils, weapons, footwear, snow-shoes, chessmen and many other articles—in great quantity and variety.

Novgorod's accumulation of wealth and wide-ranging connections with the whole of the civilised world of the day led to a rapid spiritual development and a rapid growth of art and culture, in particular the art of building. It is noteworthy, too, that the whole population of the city—from the Prince and the Archbishop to the least of the townsfolk—were involved in this building activity in one way or another.

"Lord Novgorod the Great": by this title the city was known throughout the land of Rus. Why, we may ask, was this honour not paid to Kiev, or Vladimir, or any other city? The essential difference was that Novgorod recognised no other lord and master than itself: it was the first republic of the mediaeval period in Russia. The Princes ruled as sovereigns of Novgorod only until the thirties of the 12th century: thereafter they were merely military commanders whose actions were subject to the control of the popular assembly, the *Veche*. If a Prince broke his agreement with the *Veche* he was dismissed, and someone else took his place; and the *Veche* maintained a similar control over other elected dignitaries. It is true that in the 14th century the boyars, led by the Mayor and the Archbishop, succeeded in gaining mastery of the popular assembly; but even at this period the common people were sometimes able to regain control of the *Veche*. Sometimes, also, two rival assemblies met at the same time; and this commonly led to the destruction of a few boyars' mansions, a hand-to-hand fight on the bridge over the Volkhov or, at the very least, a street brawl. Risings of the townspeople were also of frequent occurrence: between the middle of the 12th century and the end of the 15th there were more than eighty.

In short, life in Novgorod was freer than in other mediaeval Russian cities. It was no accident that the first Russian heresies developed here. Nor is it unexpected to find one of the favourite heroes of the Novgorod *byliny*, Vaska Buslaev, proclaiming that he has faith neither in dreams, nor in sneezes, nor in the croaking of ravens, nor in any other portents, but only in his own valour and daring—an independence of mind which is unprecedented in the feudal world.

The art of Novgorod reflects not only certain specific features of the city's historical development and of its social and political life but also the practical, matter-of-fact cast of mind of the citizens of mediaeval Novgorod. The architecture of Novgorod, for example, is not given to magnificence or elegant refinement; and the figures which look down on us from the icons are usually those of the patron saints of commerce and the various crafts, and of the different aspects of economic life. In short the art of mediaeval Novgorod is closely related to the needs of everyday life and the daily concerns of the citizens.

For us who live in the 20th century the artistic culture of Novgorod has a particular interest. During the terrible years of the *Tatarshchina*, when the land was red with the glow of fires and once-flourishing cities lay in shapeless heaps of rubble, the artistic life of Russia was almost completely wiped out. Here and there, perhaps, a spark still smouldered under the ashes—no more than smouldered, for in those days men were mainly concerned about the roof over their heads, their daily bread, and the good sword they wielded. Only in Novgorod was it otherwise. The dense forests which surrounded the city, and the network of swamps, rivers and streams which flooded the countryside in the spring spates, provided an almost impregnable defence against the Tatars, Novgorod's artistic development

ѲЕДИЗ　　　　　ＡΠОСЪ

ГЕѠРГИ　　　　　ВЛАСИ

was hampered but not brought to a halt by the onslaught of Baty and his Mongols. For our knowledge of Russian art in the 13th and even the 14th century, therefore, we must depend mainly on the work produced in Novgorod, which has come down to us in incomparably greater quantity than the arts of other parts of Russia, and has accordingly been the subject of much more intensive study. Novgorod, the "new city", is in fact one of the oldest cities in Russia; almost as old as Kiev. No doubt it was given this name by comparison with the older fortified settlement established by the Slavs of the Lake Ilmen area.

By the 12th century Novgorod was a bustling commercial town which had spread to both banks of the Volkhov. The left bank, with the *kreml* or citadel and the Cathedral of St Sophia, was known as the "St Sophia Quarter"; the right bank, with the market and the square in which the *Veche* met, as the "Commercial Quarter". The two parts of the town were linked by a timber bridge over the Volkhov.

Unlike the cities of Kievan Rus and Vladimir-Suzdal—which were a confused huddle of stone and timber buildings, mud huts and semi-underground houses—Novgorod was mainly built of timber. The only stone structures were the walls and towers which protected the city from attack and the many churches; but these isolated stone buildings were lost in a sea of timber houses. Of timber, too—as we learn from a local chronicler—was the first Christian church built in the town, the Church of St Sophia (989), of which no trace has survived.

Novgorod was—by the standards of the time, at least—well provided with amenities. It had, for example, a water supply system of a rather primitive kind; excavation has shown that as early as the 10th century timber paving was beginning to appear; and by the 11th century all the streets were paved. The *Yaroslavova Pravda*, the first written code of Russian law, refers to the "roadmaking duty" as obligatory for all: the Prince was required to pave a given stretch of road, the Archbishop was responsible for another, and similarly with the boyars, the merchants, and even foreigners resident in the town.

The wide, level streets were lined with solid timber houses roofed with boarding, often of two stories. The ground floor or basement was not heated and served as a store-room. The houses were set back from the street behind a paling, and to the rear were timber-paved courtyards with various domestic offices.

The streets of Novgorod were filled all day long with noisy, bustling life. This activity began very early in the morning: at six o'clock the bells of the countless churches sounded the call to matins, the shutters of the shopkeepers' booths and the warehouses were thrown open, and the first wisps of smoke began to curl into the air above the houses. To the chimes of the bells were added the clang of the blacksmiths' hammers, the screeching of saws, the rumble of carts and the voices of the shopkeepers crying their wares. As the day wore on the streets and the market-place were filled with a ceaseless flow of people—thrifty housewives hurrying to buy provisions from the hawkers' trays, foreign visitors vainly trying to explain something to a craftsman much the worse for liquor, peasants walking with unhurried step alongside their carts. Then suddenly there would resound urgently through the town the rapid tolling of a bell and, abandoning at once whatever they were doing, the citizens would pour through the streets to the Assembly Square. This square, in the Commercial Quarter, had once been occupied by the palace of Yaroslav the Wise (the memory of which is preserved in the Scandinavian sagas). By the middle of the 12th century the site of the palace was occupied by the Assembly Bell and the rostrum from which the *posadnik* (mayor) and the military leaders of Novgorod addressed the citizens, and on which the Princes kissed a cross and swore allegiance to Lord Novgorod the Great.

On feast days a great silence settled on the city, broken only by the pealing of the bells as the people of Novgorod walked sedately to the city's many churches. Of these the largest and the oldest was the Cathedral of St Sophia, built by Prince Vladimir, son of Yaroslav, between 1045 and 1050. The name of the cathedral and the fact that it stood in the *kreml* suggest that its builders were seeking to imitate the architecture of Kiev under its Grand Princes; but this was not in fact the case. The cathedral is built in roughly dressed local stone with a small amount of brick, and has five domes, with a sixth over the stair-tower. The arrangement of large masses, the small number of windows and the absence of any ornament on the walls combine with the considerable dimensions of the cathedra to create an impression of austerity and dignified simplicity.

The style of the interior matched that of the exterior. It was simple, severe, and quite lacking in the luxuriant ornament found in the Cathedral of St Sophia in Kiev. Mosaic decoration, for example, was employed only in the central apse and in the flooring. For some unknown reason the church was not painted until the 12th century: the work is referred to by the chronicler in the years 1108 and 1144. There is, however, one fragment of painting – a representation of SS. Constantine and Helena in the south porch, in an *al secco* technique rarely found in Russia at this period – which most scholars are inclined to date as early as the 11th century.

From the 12th century, when Novgorod became a republic ruled by the *Veche*, St Sophia was the principal church of the city. Dominating the town and the surrounding district, it seemed to symbolise the power and spiritual magnificence of Novgorod. Within the precincts of the church were established a magnificent library and a school. Here the local chroniclers began to record the history of their town, and within these walls were preserved splendid works of art and craftsmanship (including jewellery manufactured both in Novgorod and in other cities), the study of which might enable the local artists to perfect their skills. Finally St Sophia was used for the reception of foreign ambassadors and other visitors, and its galleries and vaults provided safe keeping for the city treasury.

In the first quarter of the 12th century a number of large churches were also built in the Commercial Quarter, and building continued on the left bank of the Volkhov. The most original building belonging to this period is the Cathedral of St George (1119), in the princely Yuryev Monastery (the Monastery of St George). Its stair-tower is built as a direct continuation of the west front, forming a rectangular projection only on the north side. The result was to produce an unusual arrangement of the domes: if these are joined by imaginary straight lines they form a triangle whose vertex lies slightly to one side, above the tower.

We can gather that the citizens of Novgorod were proud of this church, for the local chronicler, who is very sparing of references to individuals, records in his account of the building of the Cathedral of St George that "Master Peter laboured on this work".

In the thirties of the 12th century a rising which had long been brewing came to a head at last, and many were the citizens who lost their lives in street clashes or were thrown from the Volkhov

bridge into the river. The princedom of Novgorod was transformed into a republic of boyars and merchants ruled by a popular assembly. The *kreml* now became the residence of the Archbishop and the Mayor, the leading personalities of the city, while the Princes moved to the old fortress of Rurik, where a *terem* (tower, keep) had been built in 1103.

The last princely church to be built in Novgorod was the Church of the Saviour on the Nereditsa (1198) *(Plate p. 70)*. This is a very different type of building from the grandiose cathedrals of the 11th and 12th centuries. It is a small whitewashed church with a single dome, a plain façade divided into three parts, and three apses, the two lateral apses being much lower than the central one. All the lines of the building are uneven and irregular, almost as if moulded freehand. For a building of such small size the walls are unnecessarily thick. In the west front is an entrance leading up to the gallery, supported not on vaulting but on wooden joists, which opens into the space under the dome only on the west side.

The interior of the church was decorated with paintings, on the usual subjects—illustrations of the Gospels and figures of prophets, celestial warriors and men of God. These sturdy broad-shouldered figures with rugged, austere faces, directing a piercing stare on the worshippers below or contemplating them mournfully from under lowered eyelids, seemed to be urging them to repentance with every fibre of their body and reminding them of the approach of the great Judgment Day—of which there was a grandiose representation on the west wall of the church.

The great company represented on the walls was not, however, confined exclusively to men of the Church. In the centre of the west wall was a portrait of the founder of the Nereditsa Church, Prince Yaroslav, offering a model of his church to Christ enthroned *(Plate p. 69)*.

Until the second world war the Nereditsa was almost the only mediaeval church in the whole of Europe which still preserved its painted decoration intact. Its destruction is an irreparable loss both to art historians and to lovers of art. When the German army was attacking Novgorod its artillery bombarded the Nereditsa at point-blank range, and the church was completely ruined. After the war it was rebuilt; but there could be no question of restoring the 12th century paintings which had been reduced to dust and ashes.

The modest architecture of the Nereditsa Church indicates that the Prince's treasury was now in low water; and it also points to another, much more important, fact—the increasing democratisation of taste. The boyars and merchants now frequently joined with the inhabitants of a particular street or district to carry out building work; and this widening of the architects' clientèle inevitably led to compromises in design. The churches were now smaller, almost square in plan, with a single dome supported on four piers. The stair-towers disappeared, and the open galleries gave place to closed chambers, in one of which was a kind of private chapel dedicated to the donor's patron saint. The Nereditsa is a typical example of this style of church.

Many churches were built by craft corporations or "brotherhoods" and by merchants' guilds. The chroniclers could barely keep pace with the new building: foundations of new churches might have to be recorded several times a year. Some of the merchants' churches were used as a place for keeping their business accounts, or standard weights and measures, or their most precious wares; for the stout stone walls of the churches provided greater security than the timber-walled store-rooms in their houses. And it was natural that when the structure of the church was put to such practical uses no one should be concerned about the beauty of the architecture or the decoration of the walls: the church had merely to provide accommodation for the faithful of the parish and to be stoutly and strongly built.

Then came the 13th century and the Mongol invasion. As we have seen, Novgorod escaped the worst of the devastation wrought by the Tatars in Russia; but it was, nevertheless, indirectly affected by the invasion. Moreover it had troubles of its own—the struggle with the Swedes and the knights of the Teutonic Order, which ended only with the victories of Alexander Nevsky (the Battle of the Neva in 1240 and the "Battle on the Ice" on Lake Peipus in 1243). Accordingly between the thirties and forties of the 13th century and the beginning of the 14th the artistic life of Novgorod was at a low ebb. This is particularly evident in architecture, for in the prevailing atmosphere of gloom and uncertainty about the future people had neither the resources nor the desire to build on the same scale as in earlier times. The main building effort was concentrated on fortifications, and the only churches recorded by the chroniclers as having been erected between 1240 and 1290 are three modest wooden structures.

In the 14th century, however, Lord Novgorod the Great enjoyed a fresh period of prosperity. Convoys of merchant ships again sailed the seas, and as in earlier times Novgorod despatched naval escorts to meet foreign traders and accompany them from Lake Ladoga up the River Volkhov to the city. From this period until the middle of the 15th century Novgorod once again became one of the most powerful and most prosperous of Russian cities.

In art the first signs of this revival can be seen in the closing years of the 13th century, with the building of the Church of St Nicholas-in-Lipna at the mouth of the River Msta on Lake Ilmen. (The name comes from the old Slavonic word *lipna*, a swamp or bog: the church was surrounded by swamp land). Some of its architectural features—the roof borne on a trefoil arch with a much heightened middle section, the absence of subdivisions in the external walls, the single squat apse, the single dome—represent the beginning of a new period in the history of the architecture of Novgorod.

The Church of the Dormition at Volotovo,[4] built in 1352 (and destroyed during the second world war), reproduced the same type with only minor changes; and this trend was further developed in the Church of St Theodore Stratilates (1361) and the Church of the Transfiguration in the Commercial Quarter (1374) *(Plate p. 75)*.

Apart from the fact that St Theodore's roof is borne on a trefoil arch, while the Transfiguration has a hipped roof with four gables, both churches are remarkably similar. Both of them have a single dome, a single apse and a tripartite division of the external walls, and both—rather unexpectedly for Novgorod—are of considerable elegance. The apses are decorated with slender colonnettes linked by arches; under the domes are bands of dentils and triangular indentations; above the windows are semicircular ribs like eyebrows; and scattered about the walls, with no regard for symmetry, are a variety of rosettes and crosses, either carved in relief or hollowed out of the wall, and niches of varying shapes and sizes. The decoration undoubtedly shows the influence of ornament carved from wood.

Both churches were so much to the taste of the citizens of Novgorod that many contemporary and later buildings either imitated them or were mere variations of the same type. But with the exception of the Church of SS. Peter and Paul at Kozhevniki (1406) all these churches fall short of their models: one seems too wide for its height, in another the dome appears unduly massive, and so on.

We learn from the chronicler that the Church of the Transfiguration was decorated with paintings by Theophanes the Greek (Feofan Grek). Before coming to Russia Theophanes, a Byzantine by origin, had worked in Constantinople, Galata, Chalcedon and Caffa (Feodosiya in the Crimea), where he was said to have decorated more than forty churches. In Russia he worked in Novgorod and, at the beginning of the 15th century, in Moscow. The only wall paintings which can be ascribed to him with complete confidence, however, are the frescoes in the Church of the Transfiguration.

Theophanes was a bold and spirited artist; and it was remarked by contemporaries that he never painted from models, as was the accepted practice of the day, but relied entirely on his soaring imagination. Whether he was painting youthful angels or grey-haired hermits, his figures were filled with an intense inner life: sometimes sorrowing, sometimes absorbed in contemplation, they speak directly to us in the wordless language of painting.

Theophanes has a very individual style, highly generalised, almost impressionistic. He was fond of warm tones of yellow and brownish-orange (in faces, hands, clothing, or haloes) against a contrasting ground painted in shades of cold greyish-blue, greyish-green or greyish-violet. He rendered masses not only by the use of deep shadows but also by bold lines of white emphasising the areas of greatest relief.

One of the most impressive pieces of painting in the Church of the Transfiguration is the figure of St Macarius the Egyptian *(Plate p. 72)*. He is represented as a majestic old man with his hands raised in the gesture of prayer. His swarthy face stands out against the mass of white hair which falls to his shoulders and merges with his long grey beard. Under his sorrowfully knitted brows, which cast a shadow over almost the whole of the upper part of his face, his eyes shine from behind half-lowered lids, giving a melancholy austerity to his glance. The pose in full face, the severely vertical lines of the figure and the exact correspondence between the positions of the two hands create an impression of immobility, of serene solemnity, which is in sharp contrast with the internal tension expressed in the face and the eyes. We feel the great force of this inspired figure, which owes its effect mainly to Theophanes' free and impressionistic manner. The bold strokes which delineate the hair, the beard and the clothing of this saintly hermit seem to have been drawn by the hand of a giant.

An artist of powerful and individual talent and at the same time a man of wide culture, Theophanes made a great impression on his contemporaries. All who came into contact with this gifted painter were hard put to it to decide which was the more remarkable—his dexterity with the brush, his powerful imagination, his vigorous personality or the good sense of his discourse.

In any account of the art of mediaeval Novgorod icon-painting must occupy a special place. We possess considerable numbers of icons from this period; and indeed, as we have already noted, it is mainly from them that we draw our knowledge of the development of Russian painting in the 13th and 14th centuries. The word icon is derived from the Greek *eikon*, an image or representation. Icons

were painted on wooden panels, which in the case of larger works might be built up from a number of separate boards joined by wooden pins and dowels. On the front of the panel a rectangular cavity known as the "ark" or "shrine" was hollowed out, leaving a slightly raised rim which served as a kind of frame. Then the panel was covered, either in whole or in part, with canvas, and on top of this was applied a ground coat made from a mixture of powdered alabaster or chalk and animal glue. On this the painting was done in tempera (i.e., with colours based on an egg-yolk medium). The colours were used either in the pure state or mixed to produce various shades; much use was also made of gilding.

It is scarcely necessary to enumerate the range of subjects depicted in icons, for these are fairly generally known: we shall merely note, as occasion arises, certain subjects which fall outside the usual repertoire. At the outset, however, one significant point must be referred to—the fact that the icons representing saints almost outnumber all the others put together. The reason for this is clear. To the people of the period with which we are concerned the saints were intermediaries between them and God, ever ready to intervene on their behalf and to intercede for them. Invisible, usually benevolent but occasionally terrible in their wrath, the saints were always at a man's side, taking the liveliest interest in all his worldly concerns throughout his life from the cradle to the grave.

When a child was born, therefore, its parents hastened to have it baptised within a week—for one never knows what mishap may befall a child and the Devil is always lying in wait for an unchristened soul. The child was given the name of a saint, usually the saint on whose day the christening took place, and thereafter it had its own guardian angel, ready until its dying day to preserve it from all ills.

Then as time went on childhood passed into adolescence, and soon it was necessary to decide what business or trade a youth should follow. But when a man of the Middle Ages chose a particular occupation he acquired another patron saint—sometimes, indeed, two. If he decided to become a blacksmith or a doctor he came under the protection of SS. Cosmas and Damian; the patron of carpenters and boatwrights was St Nicholas, of well-diggers St Theodore Tiro or St Theodore Stratilates. The protector of gardeners was St Spiridion, of stock-rearers St Blaise (Vlasy), the ancient Slav "cattle god" Veles now transformed into a Christian saint and retaining the same functions as in his pagan incarnation. The particular duties assigned to certain saints were remarkably varied. St George the Victorious, for example, was the guardian of ploughmen and shepherds; but he was also the patron of all Russian warriors, so that his cult achieved particular popularity during the struggle with the Mongols. In a word, all forms of human activity were at this period under the protection of the saints. Even the horse-coper had his own particular patron, St Parasceve or St Pyatnitsa ("St Friday"). St Parasceve—together with St Anastasia, with whom she was often represented—was also responsible for trade and commerce, and accordingly churches dedicated to her were built in the market-places of the mediaeval Russian cities; and, by the same token, fairs were held on Fridays. St Parasceve also had certain duties more appropriate to her sex, for she was regarded as the patron saint of women's domestic tasks. And woe betide any over-industrious housewife who sat up until midnight on Friday at her spinning instead of paying honour to her patroness on her own particular day! For then St Parasceve would cause sleep to overcome her unfaithful servant and would plague her by throwing ashes and flax-combings into her eyes.

When anything went wrong in a man's household or business he appealed at once for the help of the saints. If a thief broke in by night St Theodore Tiro was applied to for the return of the stolen property. If the hens were laying badly St Mamas would be asked for help; if the cow fell sick it was a matter for St Blaise. The mediaeval saints thus took on their shoulders all the worries and anxieties of the ordinary people who looked to them for assistance and protection.

The folk calendar, and with it the regular round of work in the household and in the fields, was built up round a succession of saints' days, and this is reflected in a whole series of proverbs and popular saws. "St Dmitry needs no ferryman", was one old saying: this meant that from the 26th October, St Dmitry's name-day, the rivers could be expected to freeze. On St George's Day, 23rd April, the cattle were driven out to pasture for the first time after the winter: hence the saying, "St George comes in with the grass". The careless peasant who had not laid in a store of hay in good time knew that his last chance was on St Procopius' Day, 8th July, the latest possible day for haymaking. In consequence the unfortunate saint acquired the rather disparaging nickname of St Procopius Lazy-Scythe. We find the same kind of thing in the kitchen and backyard. "Cut your cabbages—don't wait for the Protection" (the feast of the Protection of the Virgin, 1st October) was the admonition addressed by zealous housewives to their younger and less conscientious sisters. And an abundance of similar examples could be quoted from all the varied activities of human life.

It is easy, therefore, to see why icons were of such importance to the people of this period. They were not found only in churches, but were an essential element in the furnishing of every dwelling house, from a prince's mansion to the meanest peasant's hut. The number and artistic quality of the icons in a man's house were taken as an indication of his degree of prosperity in the same way as, for example, the number of gold and silver vessels displayed on his sideboard.

The icons were hung in rows in a special corner of the living room. Each one was covered with a screen to protect it from the dust, and the whole corner was draped with a curtain of heavy, solid material. In a wealthy household the edges and background of an icon were covered with an *oklad* (frame) of gold or silver, embossed or chased. Below the icons were splendid hangings, usually of satin, embroidered with silk and metal brocade and pearls. The corner with the icons was a central feature of the house, as is indicated by its popular name of *krasny kut*, the "fair corner".

The houses of the wealthy contained a special room known as the "room of the Cross", one wall of which was completely covered with icons. When the owner of the house had a domestic chaplain divine service was celebrated in this room.

Icons were also hung at the entrances of houses in order to ensure divine protection for the occupants; on the gates of stables in order that SS. Florus and Laurus, the saintly horse-breeders, might drive away the mischievous imps who tied elf-knots in the horses' manes; on wells, so that St Theodore Tiro (or his twin, St Theodore Stratilates), spear at the ready, might keep a watchful eye on the watersprite, lest he should carry off some thoughtless woman come to draw water. At crossroads, special posts were erected on which icons were mounted under a protective roof; for it was well known that the Evil One was accustomed to lurk about such places under cover of night.

In the popular mind the saint and his representation on an icon were inseparably linked: the icon was a kind of materialised image of the saint. If a worshipper's prayers were answered he would express his gratitude to the icon in suitable fashion: a man of small means might offer a candle costing three *altyns*, a more prosperous citizen might present a string of coloured beads or an embroidered pall, or perhaps a costly *oklad* for the icon. But if a prayer went unheard the icon might be "punished" by the removal of its *oklad* and decorative hangings, or even by having its face turned to the wall.

This matter-of-fact and businesslike attitude led to a very considerable demand for icons. In the 16th and 17th centuries, and perhaps even earlier, there were special stalls for icons in the market-places, at which a purchaser might acquire any particular icon which took his fancy. To talk of buying and selling, however, was regarded as unseemly; for a man who "bought" an icon would have been regarded as buying the saint himself. The convention, therefore, was to say that the icon had been "exchanged for money". If the seller thought that the customer was not offering enough he would push the money away without saying a word; and the process would continue until the two parties finally reached agreement on a price.

The owners of icons of high artistic quality treated them as cherished possessions, making special mention of them in their wills along with objects made of the precious metals. They were presented to the Tsar on the name-day of his patron saint, on the birth of an heir to the throne, and on other special occasions; and they were also offered to highly-placed officials and other important personages as a mark of high respect.

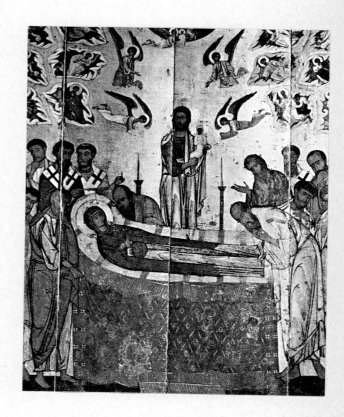

Icons do not as a rule make an immediate appeal to the modern eye on account of the distinctive features of their representational language, in which everything turns on a special system of symbolism. This was to be expected in a period when the most ordinary phenomena of life were construed as good or bad omens, when the whole visible universe and the whole history of mankind were interpreted as a gigantic pattern of symbols. In mediaeval painting almost every figure, in addition to its immediate representational significance, also had another meaning—Christ or the Virgin, the Christian Church or one of the sacraments, or some particular idea or event. Thus the three Kings in the Nativity personified the three ages of man—youth, maturity and old age—and were depicted accordingly in the icons. And again there was a symbolic idea behind this personification: all mankind, young and old, were called on to worship Christ. The gifts brought by the three Kings were also symbolical: they offered the Child "gold, as to a king; frankincense, as to God; and myrrh, as to a dead man". Many other scenes represented in icons were also of symbolic significance: the Fall and the Expulsion from Paradise, for example, represented the redeeming sacrifice of Christ. Even the placing of the figures had its own symbolism: thus in the Last Judgment the foolish virgins symbolised the rejected sinners and stood on Christ's left, while the wise virgins represented the blessed and were placed on His right hand. Finally there was a whole symbolism of gesture: a hand pressed against the cheek indicated grief, while a hand held out with open palm was a sign of submission. There were also a great variety of attributes associated with particular figures. Angels would often have pilgrims' staffs in their hands, indicating their rôle as divine messengers; martyrs had crosses, as a sign that they had suffered for the Faith; bishops carried the Gospels; prophets had scrolls of documents; and the magnanimous and benevolent SS. Cosmas and Damian could be recognised as doctors from the boxes of medicine they carried. It would be easy to multiply the examples.

Symbolism, indeed, runs through the whole of mediaeval painting. In many Novgorod icons of the 13th and 14th centuries one of the figures is represented on a much larger scale than the others—sometimes because he is the leading figure in the scene (in the case of St John, St George and St Blaise, for example) *(Plate p. 71)*, sometimes because he also personifies the victory of the forces of light over the forces of darkness (e.g., St George in the icons representing "St George and the Dragon") *(Plate p. 82)*. And again many other examples could be quoted.

This symbolism of ideas leads to a symbolism of artistic expression. When the icon-painter requires to indicate a particular locality he employs a whole system of distinguishing marks, using the part to represent the whole. A blue segment sprinkled with gold dots in the upper part of a picture represents the firmament with its spangle of stars. Two trees—sometimes only one—serve to represent a forest or, in some cases, the Earthly Paradise; a small tower stands for a palace, a battlemented wall for a town. If a character is seated on a stool, or is associated with a table or some other item of domestic furnishing, this indicates that the action is taking place indoors. Sometimes, to put the matter beyond doubt, the artist paints a little tower or house, covered with drapery, *(velum)*, on either side of the central figure.

One of the principal conventions of mediaeval painting is the method of representing the succession of events in time. The method of representation is of necessity conventional, for the expression of the passage of time lies quite outside the proper scope of painting. The painter is concerned not with temporal but with spatial relationships: he can show the development of an action in space but not in time. The mediaeval icon-painter, bringing together into a single moment of time a series of events which took place over a period, crowding into a restricted space the whole wide expanse of the world, combines in a single composition a variety of episodes from a particular story, showing what took place before the principal event and what came after it. Moreover in representing the characters involved in these various episodes he may sometimes disregard the proper sequence of events, mingling earlier occurrences with later or showing the same characters several times. Thus in icons of the Nativity we see a whole series of events represented simultaneously—the Nativity itself, the angels telling the good tidings to the shepherds, the three Kings travelling from the East, Joseph in the desert talking to a herdsman, and, finally, midwives preparing to bathe the Child. (There is a magnificent 15th century icon from Novgorod on this subject in the Tretyakov Gallery). Nor did anyone take it amiss if an icon showed Jerusalem situated close to Constantinople, or even to Moscow; for the mediaeval Russian icon-painter (and for that matter his contemporaries in western Europe) had no conception of time or of distance.

Another important characteristic is that the icon-painters—and indeed mediaeval painters in general—strove to represent their subjects in a single plane. They achieved this in a variety of ways, but principally by the use of inverse perspective. The technique is based on a genuine reversed perspective and is not merely a distorted version of regular linear perspective. In using it the artist was governed by a set of definite rules: the difference was that the vanishing point was not in the background of the picture but out in front, as if it were in the eye of the person looking at the picture. In consequence the objects represented did not appear smaller as they receded into the background—as they do in modern painting and in the real world—but grew larger. In other words, in icon-painting volumes and distances are, as it were, turned inside out. The effect of a single plane is obtained also by making figures in the foreground and the background of the same size: indeed the more distant figures are sometimes larger than the nearer.

Finally we come to what is perhaps the most important element in painting—the use of colour. The icon-painter used flat primary colours, with no variation of tone over the painted area. Such colours always produce the impression of a plane surface, particularly where they show no variation in luminosity—that is, where the artist does not use darker or lighter tones. The combination of large surfaces evenly covered with flat colours is one of the principal means of achieving a uniform pattern in a single plane—an effect based on the arrangement of all the figures and objects represented in the picture. For the icon-painter this technique is a source of unity and harmony, and consequently of beauty. The reader must not, however, suppose that this flatness of the decorative surface is a purely formal effect. On the contrary, it contributes to the revelation of the content; for the concordance of forms and colours, combined with the rhythmic unity, is one of the most effective means of linking the different figures in a composition.

These features of the icon-painters' technique are a reflection of mediaeval patterns of thought, with their abstractness, their symbolism, and their desire to ensure that the sacred events represented in these paintings were set apart from the regular round of everyday life. It was a very understandable desire, for the heroes represented by the mediaeval painter were very unlike ordinary people. They lived in a world of signs and wonders, and could themselves work wonders: they were indifferent to the joys of earthly life; they could read the thoughts in men's minds, they understood the language of animals and birds, and the secrets of the future were known to them. An ordinary mortal could not but feel the infinite distance which separated him from the saint looking down on him from an icon. For if the saint had been no different from an ordinary man, where would his special virtue have lain, and how could he have been of any help to men in the trials and sorrows of their life on earth? Hence the artistic canons laid down by the Church for the icon-painter, the obligatory system of iconography, the practice of painting from models or from "painters' guides" *(podlinniki)*. The model was often provided by some particularly famous icon, but there were also special iconographical handbooks or guides.

Of particular interest are the "illustrated guides". These are arranged according to the regular sequence of the months in the year, beginning with September (the first month in the ancient Russian year), the days of the month and the days of the week. On each page the various festivals and saints are shown under the appropriate dates. The figures are represented in outline, with some indication also of the internal outlines—the features, the details and the folds of the clothing, with a light monotone shading to render the volumes. Short notes on each picture draw attention to particular characteristics of the type or to the colours used in the clothing. The icon-painter had a guide of this kind in front of him as he worked. To paint without a model was something quite out of the ordinary: we remember, for example, how a contemporary, discussing the artistic technique of Theophanes the Greek, remarked particularly on the fact that he did not follow any model.

Thus, from whatever aspect we consider it, Russian icon-painting was a highly conventional art. We must not forget, however, that the artist was a sentient human being who was not blind to the world which surrounded him; and wherever it was possible without prejudice to the central conception of his work and his personal artistic vision, and without departing from the strict requirements of ecclesiastical doctrine, he incorporated in his painting some particle of the real world, some feature observed in his everyday experience. He did this right up to the end of the 16th century—admittedly on a very small scale, perhaps even unconsciously; but he did it none the less, as the reader can readily see from the illustrations.

In discussing the work of the icon-painters of Novgorod we need say little about the icons of the 12th century, which—like those produced in other parts of Russia at this period—are to a greater or lesser extent under Byzantine influence. With rare exceptions they all show the same swarthy faces of Oriental cast with large dark eyes, either severe or sorrowful, the same rather sombre colouring in which various shades of ochre predominate. It is characteristic of the 12th century icons that they show only one or two figures against a plain background. Fixed in their rigid poses for all eternity, indifferent to one another and to the whole surrounding world, these figures seem to be suspended in a vacuum, an empty space painted in gold or silver, or sometimes coloured. This is the standard style of the period, and there are very few departures from it *(Plate p. 44)*.

In the 13th century, however—at an earlier period than in other Russian towns—there grew up in Novgorod a local school of icon-painting with its own distinctive characteristics. As we have noted, Novgorod did not suffer from the Mongol invasion to the same extent as other parts of Russia; and icon-painting in particular continued to develop there throughout these years of tribulation. Indeed— paradoxical though it may seem at first sight—the Mongol invasion itself promoted the rapid development of a local school in Novgorod, since it led to the interruption of the long-standing links between

90

Novgorod and Byzantium. As a result the local painters, freed from the artistic dominance of Constantinople, were compelled to rely only on their own personal judgments and standards, and to adapt their style to local preferences: and as time went on these local trends became still more firmly established. During the 13th century the faces of the saints in the icons begin to take on definite Russian characteristics, and sometimes even exhibit a distinctive Novgorod type. The smooth Byzantine manner gives place to a more vigorous style—one which is sometimes rather crude but is always expressive. Sharp colour contrasts are sometimes met with—for example red and greenish-blue. A ground colour of bright cinnabar red now came into use, and became so popular that it is found right into the 15th century.

The great period of Novgorod icon-painting was in the 14th and 15th centuries. Bright, joyous colours replace the restrained, austere hues of the earlier period. The figures of saints in individual icons increase in number and are reduced in size. Representations of particular scenes become increasingly popular; and it is noteworthy that the vigorous activity of the men of Novgorod is reflected in a similar vigour in their saints. In the icons belonging to these centuries the figures are represented in motion, in a range of different—though not very varied—activities and attitudes. Each of these figures is engaged in some particular action: Abraham and Sarah busy themselves with the entertainment of the three angels *(Plate p. 89)*, St George rides full tilt at the dragon *(Plate p. 82)*, St Nikita (Nicetas) thrashes a demon with a cudgel, Jesus leads Adam and Eve out of the fiery furnace, and so on. The plain monotone backgrounds have disappeared, at least in representations of particular scenes. The citizens of Novgorod in this period were not fond of the diffuse and indefinite, and the icon-painter sought, while preserving the characteristics we have already discussed, to indicate the setting of the action; and accordingly buildings, trees and rocky caverns now begin to appear in the background of the icons. Backgrounds consisting of a plain paint wash are found only in icons forming part of a set or tier *(chin)* on an iconostasis, for example a *deesis* or a company of prophets. As instances we may take the icons of the Archangel Michael or St Barbara *(Plate p. 79)*, who provided protection against fire or the perils of the sea (both in the Tretyakov Gallery). We may note incidentally that the Novgorod icons of the 14th century frequently show a combination of different techniques, using graphic methods in drawing the clothing and paint in the treatment of faces—a feature found, for example, in the works just mentioned.

Of special interest, however, are the icons representing particular scenes. It is in these that we find the artist bringing in details from everyday life. We may take as an example a scene from the margin of an icon devoted to the life of St George, an early work belonging to the beginning of the 14th century *(Plate p. 95)*. This represents one of the martyrdoms suffered by the saint, showing him immersed to the waist in a cauldron of boiling oil, with his hands raised in the gesture of prayer and his eyes turned up to heaven, preaching to a congregation of listeners who are outside the picture. The sermon he is preaching must be an eloquent one, for it has touched even the hardened hearts of the two tormentors who are engaged in stoking the fire under the cauldron: one of them is holding one hand to his ear, as if afraid of missing a single word, while the other is wiping away tears of emotion. And there are a wealth of similar lively touches in an icon of the Nativity of the Virgin *(Plate p. 80)* dating from the late 14th or the 15th century (now, like the St George already mentioned, in the Russian Museum in Leningrad), and in many other Novgorod icons of the same period on the same theme: a maid is carefully smoothing the mother's pillow, a nurse is bending over the cradle as if singing a lullaby, another is keeping flies away from the sleeping child with a fan; or again we see two wooden poles arched over the cradle as a support for muslin curtains—a type of cradle which is still occasionally seen today. Another curious detail may be quoted to show that icons, as well as delighting the eye of the art lover, also provide valuable information for the historian and student of manners. In the icon we have been discussing, the women who come to visit the mother are carrying gold and silver vessels; and in some representations of the Nativity of the Virgin these vessels are shown without lids and are seen to contain coins. From time immemorial it had been the custom to present a newly born infant with cups or goblets of precious metal filled with gold and silver coins. The literary sources refer to this custom in the 17th century; and the icons provide proof that the practice was known in Russia at a much earlier period—at least as early as the 14th century.

One 15th century Novgorod icon of special interest is the "Battle of the Men of Suzdal with the Men of Novgorod", formerly known as the "Miracle of the Icon of the Sign" *(Plate p. 81)*. The picture is based on a real event—the siege of Novgorod in 1169-1170 by the army of Prince Andrey Bogolyubsky of Vladimir-Suzdal; and the icon, which is divided into three registers, illustrates the various episodes of the story in proper sequence.

The chronicler tells us that shortly before the siege an angel appeared to John, Archbishop of Novgorod, telling him that the men of Novgorod would be victorious if the icon of Our Lady of the Sign were placed on the walls of the citadel. (The icons of this iconographical type represent the Virgin with her hands raised in prayer; on her breast, usually in a round medallion, is a half-length figure of a young and beardless Christ, in the same posture as His Mother). The icon-painter begins his story at the moment when the icon is carried out of the church; and since the story is concerned with a real and local event the setting is precisely defined. In the uppermost register we see the two districts of Novgorod—the St Sophia Quarter, easily recognisable from the fortifications of the citadel and the domes of the cathedral, and the Commercial Quarter, identified by the Church of the Transfiguration. The two districts are joined by the bridge over the Volkhov, shown exactly as it is described in the chronicles—built of timber, with no hand-rail, and supported on timber piers. The Archbishop hands the icon over to a deacon, and we then see them crossing the bridge, with the boyars and the people coming out of the citadel to meet them. Thus, in order to show the development of the subject in time, following the principle we have already discussed, the Prince and his clergy are represented twice in the same composition. In the middle register the story reaches its climax. The icon now stands on one of the towers of the citadel; within the walls can be seen the warriors of Novgorod, and facing them are the forces of Suzdal; and on both sides is a forest of lances and triumphantly waving banners. Three horsemen ride out from the besieging army, and three others emerge from the gates of the city to meet them. It looks as if a parley is to be held; but this is not to be. Unable to control their impatience, the men of Suzdal loose their bow-strings and a hail of fiery arrows flies against the icon. Such

blasphemy is not to be endured, and the warriors of Novgorod surge out from the citadel, led by four saintly champions—George the Victorious, SS. Boris and Gleb, and Alexander Nevsky. Their lances are pointed against the enemy, as is the naked sword borne by an angel who flies down from Heaven. The result of the battle is a foregone conclusion. The front ranks of the army of Suzdal stand their ground, and the bodies of the fallen are trampled under the hooves of the horses; but the rear ranks break and flee. This icon is the first intimation of an important stage in the development of Russian painting, the emergence of the new *genre* of the historical battle picture; for this icon is essentially a battle picture, painted according to the traditions of icon-painting merely because in the circumstances of the time there was no alternative.

The reason for the choice of such an unusual subject for an icon, and for its occurrence in Novgorod of all places (and the popularity of the theme in Novgorod in the second half of the 15th century is shown by the fact that we possess three variants of the same subject—in the Novgorod Museum, the Russian Museum in Leningrad and the Tretyakov Gallery) is of some interest. Basically the reason is a political one. Novgorod had long been resisting the centralising tendencies of Moscow, sometimes indeed going so far as to betray the wider interests of Russia: during the decisive moments of the struggle with the Mongols, for example, only Ryazan and Novgorod failed to send their forces to take part in the Battle of Kulikovo. In the 15th century, when the friction with Moscow was particularly acute, a number of literary works were produced in Novgorod celebrating the city's earlier glories and remembering the great deeds done in the past. In 1430, for example, there appeared a new literary account of the memorable battle with the men of Suzdal in the 12th century, which now included the "Tale of the Miracles of the Icon of the Sign" (unlike the earlier chronicle, which was simple and straightforward, with no miracles). This account tells how during the attack by the army of Suzdal the icon, having been hit by their arrows, shed tears and turned away from the enemy; and then "there fell darkness upon them... and blinded them, every man". The icon-painter shows us nothing of this miracle, but he does depict another—the appearance of the warrior saints, of whom there is no mention in the chronicle. The significance of this is clear: if Moscow seeks to interfere with the independence of Novgorod then she will find not only the people of Novgorod but all the hosts of Heaven ranged against her. Even the patron saint of Suzdal, Boris (who had been Prince of Rostov) was on the side of Novgorod, to say nothing of St George and Alexander Nevsky, the invincible champion of the men of Novgorod. The appearance of Alexander Nevsky on the icon is of course a complete anachronism, for he was born half a century after the siege of Novgorod by Andrey Bogolyubsky. But in the Middle Ages no one was concerned about such historical inconsistencies, particularly in works of an allegorical character.

The subject of the "Battle of the Men of Suzdal with the Men of Novgorod" and the circumstances which dictated this choice of subject make this work, of course, unique among 15th century icons. But certain features of this icon, in particular the painter's striving for a narrative effect, were to become distinctive characteristics of the painting of the following century. This interest in telling a story was so strong that we sometimes find the icon-painter introducing various details which are of purely anecdotal

significance. As an example we may take the icon of the "Miracle of St George and the Dragon", *(Plate p. 93)* of the early 16th century (now in the Russian Museum). A huge figure of St George on horseback, wearing golden armour and a flowing scarlet cloak, fills almost the whole panel; in comparison with him the other figures represented in the icon seem pigmies. This is quite as it should be, for St George is the principal character in the icon, and moreover represents the victory of Heaven over the forces of Hell. This is indicated by the right hand of God which is seen in a gesture of blessing against a segment of blue sky and by the angel who is flying down to offer the victorious saint a golden crown. On the left is a tall tower, the open galleries of which are thronged with people, and under the arch of the lowerst storey is a princess holding the tamed dragon on a halter. Against the balcony on the first floor stands a ladder, and a young man is climbing up this ladder in great haste, taking two or three rungs at a time and looking over his shoulder quickly to see whether the monster is still pursuing him. The people on the balcony hasten to pull him over the balustrade. One of them, however, cowers back, trying to pull his cloak over his face; but his curiosity overcomes his fear and he remains fixed in his pose, his face half concealed by his cloak. In the gallery on the second storey are the Prince and Princess with their whole court; and on the summit of the tower are two heralds, proclaiming with their trumpets to all the surrounding district the happy outcome of the combat. The whole work radiates a mood of triumphant celebration, which is expressed chiefly in the treatment of the theme but is reinforced by the bright clear colours, in which scarlet and emerald green predominate.

These bright colours are perhaps the only feature which recalls the icon-painting of an earlier period. Elsewhere we see the imprint of the style of Moscow (e.g., in the elegance of line, the occasional triviality of form and almost miniature-like refinement of the painting, the striving for decorative effect both in the composition as a whole and in the detail). Later Novgorod icons of the 16th and 17th centuries are sometimes very difficult to distinguish from Muscovite work. The influence of Moscow was also felt in architecture. The whole of the art of Novgorod, in fact, lost its particular regional colouring during the last two centuries of the older Russia. What, we may wonder, had caused this change?

Even in the architecture of Novgorod in the 15th century we feel that the creative urge has lost something of its former vigour. In the boyars' churches, for example, we find no more than variations on the 14th century models which had achieved such popularity. Archbishop Euthymius II (1429-1458) devoted much effort to the building of monasteries outside the city walls and to the restoration of older buildings reconstructed in later periods, which he now sought to restore to their original appearance. Almost the only really new building of the period was the Archbishop's Mansion *(Vladychnaya Palata)* (1433), the first secular building in Russia designed specifically for a public purpose. Its well-preserved Hall of Justice is of strikingly unusual construction, with a square pier in the centre supporting the groined vaulting. This first—and last—appearance of Gothic in mediaeval Russia is explained by the fact that craftsmen from the Baltic towns were associated with the master builders of Novgorod in the construction of the Mansion.

This return to the architectural types and forms of earlier centuries flowed from the same causes as the choice of subject in the icon of the "Battle of the Men of Suzdal with the Men of Novgorod": the frictions with Moscow which developed finally into open war. Matters reached such a pitch that the authorities of Novgorod put their territory under the protection of Lithuania. The moving spirit of the plot was the ambitious wife of the mayor of Novgorod, Boretsky, who is remembered in Russian history and literature as Marfa-Posadnitsa, Martha the Mayoress. The ordinary people, however, were unwilling to accept foreign overlordship. During the last siege of Novgorod by the Muscovite army in 1477 the gunners spiked the cannon on the ramparts of the city, and the townsfolk threw open the gates and swore allegiance to the Grand Prince. Sitting in the vaulted chamber of the Vladychnaya Palata, Ivan III pronounced his decree: "No assembly bell shall there be in Novgorod, no mayor shall there be; our rule shall prevail."

The people of Novgorod remained largely indifferent to the fate of Martha the Mayoress and the other conspirators; but they were much distressed by the carrying off of their Assembly Bell to Moscow. For centuries its peals had sounded over Novgorod, many a time summoning the townsfolk to rise in rebellion. The people of Novgorod revered it as a symbol which enshrined their memories of the freedom they had enjoyed in the past and their dreams of future liberation.

A poetic old legend tells the story that when the bell was being transported through the Valday Hills in a sleigh—a scene represented in a miniature of the period—it refused to leave its native soil, jumped off the sleigh and broke into a thousand little bells, the "Valday bells" which used to tinkle in horses' harness, combining with the doleful singing of the coachmen to form a music which has been heard into our own day, carrying down through the centuries the memory of Lord Novgorod the Great.

Having discussed the art of Novgorod, we must now—in spite of the limitations on our space— say something about the art of Pskov. And indeed Pskov deserves a good deal more than a mere passing mention; for the history of the city contains many notable names and many notable events. There is, for example, the beautiful Princess Olga, wife of Igor son of Rurik, Prince of Kiev, who fell in battle against the Drevlyanians, and grandmother of Vladimir "Bright Sun", whom the chronicler calls the wisest of women; and there is Alexander Nevsky, the victor in the famous Battle on the Ice. Many stories and legends are associated with this area, which in the Middle Ages lay on the western boundary of the territory of Novgorod.

Lake Peipus, on which the Battle on the Ice was fought, is joined to the Lake of Pskov by a narrow ribbon of water, and at the south end of this lake, where the River Velikaya is joined by its tributary the Pskova just before it falls into the lake, the city of Pskov was established as early as the 11th century on a high rocky promontory within its protecting ramparts (which exist to this day, though mainly in the form of a 15th century reconstruction). They are traditionally associated with the name of the fair Princess Olga; but in fact "on whose authority and by what people the city was established" even the chroniclers cannot tell.

During the early part of its history Pskov was a dependency of Novgorod, ruled by the Princes of Novgorod and their henchmen and subject in all important matters to the *Veche* of Novgorod. The city took part, however, in Novgorod's trade with the East and the West and rapidly grew rich. Then the wars with the Swedes and the knights of the Livonian Order, in which Novgorod many times left Pskov to its fate, taught the people of Pskov the love of freedom and the consciousness of their own

strength. At any rate by the middle of the 14th century Pskov had become the "younger brother of Novgorod the Great", the second feudal republic in the history of mediaeval Russia.

The works of art produced in Pskov in the 12th and 13th centuries bear witness to the city's close connections with other parts of Russia, in particular Polotsk and Smolensk, and also with Byzantium. The cathedral in the Ivanovsky Monastery, built in the first half of the 13th century, shows clearly that its architect was inspired by the work of the master builder of Novgorod, Master Peter. Even in this early period, however, the general trend of the local architecture is entirely individual and is determined by the particular circumstances of the area. Thus perhaps nowhere else in Russia were such large numbers of fortifications erected as in the Pskov area, for this was a form of building made necessary by the constant wars fought over this territory *(Plate p. 106)*. These local fortresses were known for the quality of their building: the Germans gave Izborsk, for example, the name of Eisenburg, the "iron stronghold".

The year 1348 marks the beginning of Pskov's political independence, which was to last for rather more than a hundred and fifty years. This was also the period of flowering of its art, which had now completely thrown off the influence of Novgorod. In Pskov everything was plainer and simpler than in its "elder brother", both in worldly matters and in the sphere of spiritual life. In general the Princes were of less importance in the life of Pskov, the boyars were not so rich and influential as in Novgorod, and in consequence the *Veche* had more power and the forms of government were more democratic. All this left its mark on the art of Pskov, and in particular on its architecture. Apart from the grandiose Cathedral of the Trinity (of which we have only a late 17th century reconstruction) the churches of Pskov are much simpler than those of Novgorod. They are small buildings with massive walls, usually with a single dome and a hipped roof, and with rectangular windows like ordinary houses. Their whole appearance, in fact, has something of the homeliness of a dwelling house. The rather cramped interiors of these churches are equally unassuming: usually they have no painting but are merely whitewashed. The lack of space within the churches themselves made it necessary to build on various chapels, covered porches and store-rooms; sometimes, indeed, the whole of the basement was given up to storage and similar purposes. This need cause no surprise, for the builders of the Pskov churches were for the most part the ordinary citizens of the town: churches built by boyars are of rare occurrence here. Frequently a belfry is built on to one of the annexes, or to the church itself, consisting of two or three piers supporting a crossbeam, sometimes with a pitched roof, with the bells hanging between the piers. It is these belfries which give the churches of Pskov their particular character. In this area, too, the churches were built in a matter-of-fact and easygoing way found nowhere else. The builders first built their church, and then considered to whom it should be dedicated: indeed the saint who should thus be honoured might be decided by the drawing of lots. The very names of the churches, too, strike us as familiar, almost lighthearted: the Church of St Basil the Great on the Hillock *(Plate p. 103)*, St Sergius Beyond the Ponds, St Nicholas in the Marsh, the Resurrection in the Pasture, and so on. It is significant also that there was relatively little monastery building in the territory of Pskov; and in general the monastic ideal had less influence in the sober and businesslike atmosphere that prevailed in Pskov than in other parts of mediaeval Russia.

Unlike Novgorod with its timber building, Pskov built most of its houses in stone. The material, in the form of the local flagstone, was readily at hand. The only buildings to have survived are a few 17th century merchants' houses, in particular the Pogankin House (now housing the local museum), a large two-storied building on a π-shaped plan in a severe, almost fortress-like, style of architecture. Evidently the 17th century, concerned as it was to dress up everything in the latest style, did not presume to interfere with Pskov, a city of warriors and of busy people who had no time for trifles.

Until quite recently the monumental art of Pskov was one of the least understood chapters in the history of mediaeval Russian art. The work of Soviet restorers and scholars, however, has thrown much light in these dark places. The frescoes in the cathedral of the Spaso-Mirozhsky Monastery (1156) were cleaned in 1926, and the paintings in the Church of the Nativity in the Snetogorsky Monastery in 1928-29, continuing in 1948-49. Some of the latter paintings show a strikingly original iconographic treatment, and one of the several different styles which have been identified here is curiously reminiscent of the work of a painter of a considerably later period, Theophanes the Greek. The paintings in the Church of the Nativity were apparently done soon after the building of the church, about the year 1313.

A beginning has also recently been made with the cleaning of the Pskov icons *(Plate p. 105)*, of which so far relatively few are known. In representations of particular scenes these commonly show figures in violent movement, in contrast with others which are quite motionless. The faces of the saints have a surprisingly terrestrial, almost coarse, quality. The colours most frequently used are black, red, white, dark yellow and green. It looks as if the painters of Pskov were faithful to the same ideals as the architects, preferring a style which is expressive but simple, reticent, and always closer to earth than to Heaven.

In 1510 the independence of the free city of Pskov came to an end, when with all its territories it became part of the princedom of Muscovy. The citizens of Pskov watched griefstruck as the Assembly Bell was taken down from the belfry of the Trinity Church in the citadel. Surprisingly, however, Pskov —unlike Novgorod—did not lose the distinctive features of its art when it was swallowed up in Muscovy. The churches of the 16th century can easily be taken for works of an earlier period, and the belfries of Pskov continued to be a distinctive feature of the urban scene into the 17th century.

Pskov's situation as a frontier town meant that the building of fortifications continued during the Muscovite period (or, as it would be more accurate to say, the period of a unified Russian state). In 1519 and 1524 the line of the outer city wall was continued beyond the River Pskova, and the famous Thundering Tower was built; then in the 1550s the defensive ramparts of the Pechorsky Monastery were constructed. Meanwhile, however, life flowed on in the ordinary way; within the city walls there was still the same bustle of activity in the market-place, and the craftsmen still sang as they bent over their work, just as they had done in earlier days.

V MOSCOW, THE THIRD ROME

In the first millennium A.D., as we know from archaeological excavation, there was a large Slav settlement on the banks of the River Moskva and the Yauza. Probably in the Middle Ages men laying the foundations of houses or digging into the earth for one reason or another would occasionally turn up fragments of domestic utensils, weapons or other articles used by the ancient pagan inhabitants of the area; and perhaps from time to time some trace of occupation by men of an even earlier period would come to light. But whether this happened or not, it was firmly believed in the Middle Ages that the foundation of Moscow went back to Biblical times. In the 17th century, for example, it was thought that the city had been established by Noah's grandson Moskh (Meshech) and his wife Kva; and the city's name was derived from the combination Moskh-Kva, giving Moskva, Moscow.

Moscow is first mentioned in the chronicles in the years 1147 and 1156 as a small frontier town in the Grand Princedom of Vladimir. A number of causes contributed to the city's rapid growth and increase in political importance. It stood at the junction of roads coming from the territory of Kiev and of Vladimir-Suzdal, and hundreds of thousands of refugees from the south and north-east sought shelter in the city during the Mongol invasion. Moreover there was for long (until the year 1261) no local princely dynasty in Moscow, which accordingly enjoyed a period of freedom from internal dissensions: a happy situation which also attracted large numbers of settlers fleeing from other parts of northern Russia.

By the end of the 13th and the beginning of the 14th century the territories of Moscow were among the most densely inhabited in the whole of Russia. The Princes now set about extending their domains, relying sometimes on the strength of their sword, sometimes on the depth of their purse. The son and grandson of Alexander Nevsky, Daniel and Yury, united to the princedom the cities of Pereyaslavl-

Zalessky, Kolomna and Mozhaysk; and Ivan Kalita ("Moneybags"), the great "collector of Russian territory", cast a covetous eye on the wealth of Novgorod and fought a successful war against his powerful rival the Prince of Tver. The increasing importance of the young princedom became so evident that in 1326 the residence of the Metropolitan was transferred from the ruined city of Vladimir to Moscow, and seventy years later the Muscovites received within their walls the most revered treasure in all Russia, the icon of Our Lady of Vladimir; and with the support they now enjoyed from the Church the Princes of Moscow were able to assert their superiority over the other feudal princes of Russia.

Although Ivan Kalita's reign lasted only fifteen years (1326-1341), it was a period of remarkable success. There came over the land of Rus, records the chronicler, "a great tranquillity: the Tatars ceased their attacks on Russian soil, and Christians enjoyed relief from their grievous burdens."

In this period Moscow firmly established its claim to rank as a capital city. Its external appearance, however, did not match its importance. The area occupied by the city was only a little greater than that of the present Kremlin. The houses were unpretentious wooden structures, and the churches were likewise built of timber. In spring and autumn the narrow winding streets turned into an almost impassable morass. And all round the city, buried in luxuriant vegetation in summer and in deep snowdrifts in winter, were numbers of populous villages, externally not very different from the capital city itself.

With characteristic energy Ivan Kalita set about the rebuilding of his capital. The citadel (*kreml* or Kremlin) was surrounded by massive oak palisades, behind which gleamed the domes of the churches, now built in fair white stone. These churches have not come down to us: some of them were replaced in the late 15th and early 16th centuries by more magnificent buildings with the same names and dedications, while others were demolished without replacement.

During the regency of the Metropolitan Aleksey and the reign of Dmitry of the Don (1359-1389) the area occupied by the Kremlin was extended and the wooden palisade replaced by a stone wall. From the middle of the 14th century, and particularly after the defeat of the Mongols at the battle of Kulikovo (1380), stone building—for fortifications, monasteries and churches—became general both in Moscow and in the surrounding area.

Only a very few of the many buildings of various types erected during this period have survived. No wall painting at all has been preserved. A few icons are known, but the attribution of some of them to the Moscow school is disputed.

In many respects, therefore, our knowledge of Muscovite art of the 14th and early 15th centuries is totally lacking. Such information as we have comes from the literary sources. This is explained mainly by the fact that as Moscow developed into a large and wealthy city it increasingly attracted the rapacious attentions of the Tatars, who carried out numerous raids on the city, destroying whatever they could not carry away. Much damage was also done by fires, which were a constant hazard in the congested mass of timber houses of which mediaeval Moscow was composed. The chronicler laments that in the great fire of 1364 "the whole city was burned to the very ground"; and the number of lesser fires was beyond counting.

We know from the literary sources that in the closing years of the 14th and the early years of the 15th century the painter Theophanes the Greek, with whom we are already familiar, was working in Moscow. The paintings he did in the Kremlin churches—the Cathedral of the Nativity, the Archangel Cathe-

dral and the Cathedral of the Annunciation—and in the *Terem*, the private apartments of the Grand Prince, have not been preserved; but he was clearly responsible for the icons in the *deesis* tier of the iconostasis in the Cathedral of the Annunciation, the finest of which are the figures of the Mother of God *(Plate p. 125)*, John the Forerunner and the Apostle Paul.

Another artist who worked with Theophanes the Greek on the decoration of the Cathedral of the Annunciation in 1405 was Andrey Rublëv, the greatest Russian painter of the mediaeval period. His pre-eminence is taken for granted in our own day, but it was also recognised by his contemporaries and by succeeding generations. It is surprising, therefore, to find how little information about him can be gleaned from the literary sources: even the dates of his birth and death are known only approximately.

The story of Rublëv's life as we know it today can be told very briefly. He was born in the 1360s, and was evidently a native of Moscow. While still a youth he became a monk in the Monastery of the Trinity and St Sergius (in the modern town of Zagorsk). In the nineties of the 14th century (though some scholars put the date at about 1410) he was working in Zvenigorod, in the Cathedral of the Dormition "in the Citadel" and in the Cathedral of the Nativity in the Savvino-Storozhevsky Monastery.

Evidently Rublëv's work in Zvenigorod made him known, for in 1405 we find him decorating the Cathedral of the Annunciation in Moscow along with Theophanes the Greek, and in 1408 working with Daniel the Black and "with his fellows" on the painting of frescoes and icons for the iconostasis in the Cathedral of the Dormition

in Vladimir. Both of these commissions came to him from the Grand Prince, who was not accustomed to patronise unknown or obscure artists.

How Rublëv occupied his time after his return to Moscow is not known. All that we can say is that between 1410 and 1415 he probably painted the splendid icons (formerly attributed to his period in Zvenigorod) of the saviour *(Plates pp. 137, 138)*, the Archangel Michael *(Plate p. 136)* and the Apostle Paul, and that in 1411 (or, according to an alternative view, at some time during the 1420s) he painted his most famous icon, the "Trinity". At the end of the 1420s the iconostasis in the Trinity Cathedral in the Monastery of the Trinity and St Sergius was set up; and if Rublëv did not himself take part in this work it was at least carried out under his immediate supervision. It is possible also that he may have had a hand in certain other icons, the painters of which were clearly seeking to imitate his manner *(Plates pp. 144, 145)*.

Rublëv died between 1427 and 1430, having at some time before his death painted the cathedral in the Andronikov Monastery in Moscow (though of this work nothing remains but a few pieces of ornament in the window niches). And it was in this monastery, at a very advanced age and "having these many years had honourable grey hairs", that "Andrey the icon-painter" found his eternal rest. The Andronikov Monastery *(Plates pp. 142, 143)* has now been converted into the Rublëv Museum, as a fitting tribute by posterity to this great mediaeval master.

As we have noted, Rublëv's most famous work, and indeed the most famous of all Russian icons, is his "Trinity" *(Plate p. 130)*. If we want to understand the complexity of the problems which faced the artist in this work and to appreciate the mastery with which they were solved, some preliminary explanations are required. The reader will find that the effort needed to understand this work fully will be well worth while, more particularly since most art lovers in the West are probably not familiar with this characteristically Orthodox version of the Trinity.

In mediaeval Russian painting there were three iconographical variants of the Trinity—the "Old Testament Trinity", the "Paternity" and the "New Testament Trinity". The first of these is based on a representation of three angels sitting at a table under an oak tree—the three heavenly messengers who appeared to Abraham and Sarah to tell them of the forthcoming birth of Isaac. This version is known as the "Old Testament Trinity", since the story is told in the Book of *Genesis*.

The "Paternity" shows God the Father sitting on a throne with a young, beardless Christ on his lap. Jesus is holding a sphere, and in the sphere is a white dove, representing the Holy Ghost. The "New Testament Trinity", which became popular in the 17th century, shows God the Father and Christ sitting on thrones, with the Holy Ghost hovering above them; but even in this century the more ancient "Old Testament" variant was preferred to all others. The term "Old Testament Trinity" may well strike the reader as quite inappropriate, since the doctrine of the Trinity is a dogma of Christian theology. In the Old Testament there is not, and cannot be, any mention of the Trinity. Whence, therefore, came the use of a term which can have no logical justification?

One of the basic problems facing the Church from a very early period was to combine the Old and New Testaments into an organic whole by finding a single religious conception which should link the two. For did not Christ say that he had not come to destroy the prophets but to fulfil them? It is interesting to see how this assimilation was achieved in the Middle Ages.

Certain passages in the Old Testament prophets were interpreted as references to the Immaculate Conception, the birth of Christ, His rôle as a Messiah, and so on; and most of the Old Testament stories were taken as symbolising events recorded in the New Testament. Among such episodes were the account of Abraham and Sarah entertaining the angels unawares and the story of Abraham's sacrifice. The New Testament parallels were not far to seek. The angels had foretold to the Patriarch the coming birth of Isaac, just as the archangel announced to the Virgin the birth of Christ. In order to test Abraham's faith God ordered him to sacrifice his son Isaac, and Isaac went like a lamb to the slaughter; and did not Jesus do the same in accepting death on the Cross at the will of His Heavenly Father? Such, broadly, was the reasoning of the theologians.

The artists of Byzantium and mediaeval Russia, in representing the Trinity, were in effect illustrating the Biblical text. We are told in *Genesis* that three men appeared to Abraham "in the plains of Mamre", as he "sat in the tent door in the heat of the day". Not recognising the visitors as heavenly beings, but well aware of his duty to provide hospitality, the old man bade them be seated, and gave orders for "cakes" to be baked and "a calf tender and good" to be killed for their meal. In the icons we see the angels sitting at table under an oak tree (and it will

be remembered that for the icon-painters a single tree served to represent a whole forest). We see Abraham's dwelling, but the nomad's tent has become a stone-built house represented in accordance with the conventions of icon-painting. Abraham and Sarah are shown bringing cakes to their guests, and there is frequently also a young man slaughtering the calf. Some Byzantine artists included in the same composition the scene of Abraham's sacrifice.

In this treatment of the Trinity the idea of one God in three Persons was lost: the artists found no room for it in their conception of the scene. Rublëv, a man of acute intelligence and a sensitive artist, realised this omission. In painting his icon he cut out all inessential figures and narrative detail, leaving only the table, the oak-tree, the house and the pilgrims' staffs carried by the angels—an established element of the iconographical tradition—to recall the Old Testament story. The icon shows three angels with golden hair and wings sitting at a low table. Their heads are bowed, their eyes are filled with sorrow, their lips are closed. The one in the middle is pointing enquiringly at the dish containing the head of the slaughtered calf. The gesture of the angel on the left, full of mournful solemnity, seems to confirm the inevitability of the sacrifice; and the angel on the right, as if echoing his movement, slowly lowers his hand. Everything in this picture is subordinated to the harmonious rhythm of the lines. The outlines of the angels on either side correspond exactly with the silhouette of the central figure. The angle at which the tree is bent repeats the lines of this central figure, the curve of the rock in the background matches the outline of the angel on the right, and the tiered structure of the house corresponds to the pattern formed by the body of the angel on the left.

Each of the figures in this icon represents one of the hypostases of the Trinity. This is emphasised by the different colours used in their garments— cherry red and sky blue for the angel in the middle, pinkish lilac and blue for the angel on the left, and pale green and blue for the one on the right. At the same time it is noteworthy that the garments of all three contain exactly the same shade of blue; and their faces, though there are certain barely perceptible differences between them, also show an undoubted similarity. We know with complete certainty that these three angels are indissolubly connected with one another; that they express not only their own personalities but also an essential unity. This feeling is reinforced by the composition of the icon: the three figures, sitting so closely together that their wings are touching, seem enclosed within an invisible circle which determines the whole composition.

In this work a theological conception of great complexity is given masterly artistic expression; but, as always with great art, the content of the "Trinity" has taken on characteristics which are of significance to all humanity. The arrangement of the figures in a circle, the recurrence of similar outlines, and the concentration of all glances and gestures on one object—the dish on the table *(Plate p. 132)*— emphasise the unity of thought and action which binds the three figures together. The quiet repose of the figures, the flowing rhythm of the lines, and the purity of the colours combine to create an impression of peace, tranquillity and harmony. These were precisely the qualities lacking in the world of Rublëv's day; and perhaps many of his contemporaries, as they knelt before the icon, saw in it the incarnation of the repose for which all men yearned.

Since then many centuries have passed, but for those sensitive to beauty the "Trinity" still holds its fascination. When Romain Rolland, that discerning lover of art, visited the Soviet Union in 1935 he fell under its spell. The visitors' book in the Tretyakov Gallery records his impressions: "I was delighted with the rooms filled with priceless icons. Rublëv's masterpiece will always remain in my memory as one of the most harmonious and purest of paintings."

The lessons of history had clearly demonstrated the necessity of political unification, and the battle of Kulikovo provided an instructive example of the same truth. The land of Rus was, however, still oppressed by the scourge of the feudal period—the constant internecine strife between the various princes. Thus in the 1430s there was a contest for the Muscovite throne between the Grand Prince, Vasily II, and his kinsmen Dmitry Shemyaka and Vasily Kosoy (Basil the Squint-eyed). One of the consequences of this interminably protracted struggle was the interruption of all building work in stone, for men were then too much preoccupied with other matters.

In 1462, however, Ivan III succeeded to the throne, and the situation changed completely. An adroit and far-seeing statesman and a man of boundless ambition, Ivan defeated the Princes of Yaroslav, Rostov and Beloozero, annexed Novgorod, Tver and Ryazan, and declared the Lithuanian territories which had hitherto formed part of the princedom of Kiev to belong to his ancestral patrimony. The Grand Prince of Moscow was now master of the whole of Rus, and the feudal princes were no more than great landowners who enjoyed certain special privileges. Following a practice of which history offers many examples, Ivan sought confirmation of the legitimacy of his claims in the "Tale of the Princes of Vladimir", a kind of official genealogy of the Princes of Moscow which was produced about this time. This work devotes much effort to "proving" the kinship of these princes with the Princes of Vladimir and Kiev, and tells how the Byzantine Emperor Constantine IX sent Vladimir Monomakh a royal crown, a special type of gold collar or necklace worn at coronations, and other attributes of royalty. Thereafter, says the author of the "Tale", Vladimir began to call himself Monomakh (from the Greek *monomachos* which was sometimes interpreted at this period to mean "autocrat") and "king of Great Russia". From this curious document we learn other surprising facts; for example, we are told of the bonds of kinship which linked the Princes of Moscow with such great

126

predecessors as Constantine the Great and even the Emperor Augustus. With such a genealogical tree, there could be none to cast a doubt on the noble blood of the rulers of Moscow or on their right to the title of Tsar.

Another theory which achieved great popularity, particularly among the clergy, was the idea that Moscow was the political and spiritual heir to Byzantium (which had fallen to the Turks in 1453) and the bulwark of the Orthodox East: "Moscow the Third Rome: a fourth is not to be." In 1472, when Ivan married the Byzantine princess Sophia Palaeologus, the two-headed eagle which was the symbol of the Emperors of Byzantium became the Russian national emblem.

The unifying function of Moscow was now recognised in the terms "Muscovy" and "Muscovites" which were used in the countries of the West in referring to Russia and the Russians.

These developments had their influence on the pattern of Russian art. Attention was now concentrated on the capital city, and in particular on the Kremlin; for it had to be made evident to all that this was the residence of the all-powerful ruler of these northern territories. But first, since the Kremlin still retained its function as a fortress, its defences—which by the end of the 15th century were somewhat dilapidated and ill adapted to the new methods of warfare based on the use of fire-arms—had to be reconstructed in accordance with the latest techniques of fortification.

At this period the Italians had the greatest reputation as builders, and Italian architects and craftsmen were therefore invited to work in Moscow. Men like Fioravanti, Solari, Ruffo and Alevisio were thus able to make use of Italian experience in this field for the creation of an architectural ensemble which gave expression to distinctively Russian traditions and styles.

The builders started with the walls and towers of the Kremlin, erecting tall massive ramparts with three tiers of apertures from which fire could be directed against the enemy *(Plate p. 111)*. A network of passages and chambers was contrived within the thickness of the walls, and underground tunnels were driven at suitable places to provide listening posts from which a watch could be kept on enemy attempts to undermine the defences. In addition the approaches to the fortress were defended on one side by the River Moskva and on the other by the Neglinnaya, and the two rivers were later joined by a moat. It was not surprising, therefore, that foreign ambassadors and other visitors described the Kremlin as one of the strongest fortresses in Europe. The main entrance was at the Frolovsky Tower (renamed the Spassky Tower in the 17th century, when the spire with its clocks was added) *(Plate p. 112)*. The Frolovsky Gate led into Cathedral Square, where building was carried on simultaneously with the work on the fortifications.

Between 1475 and 1479 the Cathedral of the Dormition *(Plate p. 113)* was built by the Bologna architect Ridolfo Fioravanti, who was given the name of Aristotele "by reason of his great skill at the art". The building of the cathedral had begun before Fioravanti arrived in Russia; but evidently the builders—whose names are recorded as Myshkin and Krivtsov—were of no great competence. The mortar they used was of insufficient strength, so that their work could not withstand "an earthquake which shook the city of Moscow"; and the building, which had almost reached roof level, collapsed. There soon arose in its place a new Cathedral of the Dormition, the model for which was provided by the cathedral of the same name in Vladimir. Fioravanti, however, was too good an architect to confine himself to a slavish copy of his model. Features which recall the ancient shrine of Vladimir are the plan, the stone walls (the light vaulting, however, being of brick), the subdivision of the external wall surfaces, the vaulted roof, the massive group of five domes, the narrow slit-like windows, the splayed doorways and the blind arcades which run round the whole building half-way up the walls. (The painting on the walls above the doorways dates from the 17th century) *(Plate p. 114)*. Novel features were the flattened apses, the projecting walls to the north and south of the apses, and the high plinth (now no longer visible, since the foundations of the cathedral are now considerably below ground level). The structural techniques also show new features—the use of specially made bricks, iron tie-rods, and so on.

The interior of the cathedral *(Plate p. 115)* is light and spacious. The chancel and the altar rails (which were concealed by the tall iconostasis built in the 17th century) were covered with brightly coloured frescoes. The rest of the cathedral was not painted until 1544. Of the original paintings, however, only a few fragments have survived, most of those now visible having been repainted in the middle of the 17th century. If we imagine the church as it once was, with the silver lustres hanging from the vaulting, the gold and silver vessels and the icons in their sumptuous frames, glittering with precious stones, we can understand the impression it created on contemporaries: "A church marvellous in size and height, in brightness and resonance, and of wondrous spaciousness", it was called by the proud citizens of Moscow.

And indeed the Cathedral of the Dormition was intended to convey an impression of magnificence. In those days it was the most important public building in the Kremlin, the place where solemn ceremonies were held, where Grand Princes and Tsars were crowned. Here also was the burial vault of the Metropolitan, and later of the Patriarch.

In the 1480s craftsmen from Pskov reconstructed the Cathedral of the Annunciation *(Plate p. 122)*, originally built in the 14th century, in a style which incorporated features from the architecture of Vladimir and Pskov. The original church, a small building with three domes, had now become the court church; and accordingly in 1564 galleries containing four small chapels were built round three sides and the number of domes was increased to nine.

The third of the main churches in the Kremlin *(Plate p. 119)*, the Archangel Cathedral, was rebuilt later than the others. Ivan III did not live to see it, for it was not completed until after his death, in 1509. The Italian master builder Aleviz Novy, "Alevisio the Second", allowed himself a good deal of liberty with the traditions of Russian architecture. The double row of windows and the wide cornice which runs round the church half-way up the walls give it the appearance of a two-storied building. A similar cornice cuts off the *zakomary*, the rounded pediments at the top of the gables, from the main structure of the wall; and the carved scallop-shell mouldings which cover their whole surface give the *zakomary* themselves a purely decorative significance. The mouldings in the *zakomary*, the cornices, the pilasters, the decoration of the external walls (with panels in the upper part and blind arcades in the lower), the loggia on the west front and the doorways framed in splendid carved ornament in the style of the late Italian Renaissance make the Archangel Cathedral, in spite of the traditional plan and

132

137

the group of five domes, the least Russian in spirit of all the buildings erected in the Kremlin at this period. We have only to think of it without the domes and we are reminded at once of a north Italian *palazzo*.

Of the palace buildings belonging to the reign of Ivan III the only one that has survived is the Granovitaya Palata, the Palace of Facets, built by Pietro Antonio Solari and Marco Ruffo in 1487-1491. It has a double row of windows and an almost flat roof, and above a ground floor of undecorated stonework is the façade of rusticated stone from which the palace takes its name. The interior is reminiscent of the Vladychnaya Palata in Novgorod, with a massive square pier in the centre supporting the groined vault *(Plates pp. 116-117)*. The pier is decorated with carved stone ornament, and it is thought that originally the walls were similarly carved. The walls were decorated with painting in the reign of Boris Godunov (1598-1605), but although the painting was renewed in the 17th century none of it has survived. The paintings we see today were done by artists from Palekh in 1882.

The Palace of Facets was the first public building of a secular character to be built in Muscovite Russia. Here the Princes and Tsars held counsel with their boyars, received foreign ambassadors and gave great feasts. On the occasion of a feast tables and benches were set out round the walls, and on a dais a special table was laid for the Muscovite ruler himself. Round the central pier was erected a tiered display stand, on which were exhibited great numbers of gold and silver vessels of every shape and size—cups, goblets, pitchers, and boat-shaped ladles or scoops with long curved handles. Some were no bigger than a modern coffee cup, others were so large that, in the words of Peter Petrey of Erlesund, "ducks and geese could swim in them".

The tallest structure in the Kremlin, and indeed in the whole of the mediaeval city, was the towerlike church and belfry dedicated to St John Climacus. Because of its height it was also used as a watchtower. This unusual church was built between 1505 and 1508 by the architect Bon Fryazin in place of a 14th century church of the same name. The 260 feet high tower was popularly known as "Ivan the Great" *(Plate p. 139)*, and the Cathedral Square became the Ivanovsky Square.

The building operations in the Kremlin begun during the reign of Ivan III continued in the reign of his son Vasily III. By the year 1516 the citadel of the Grand Princes of Moscow had taken on an appearance not very different from that familiar to us in later centuries. There were the same massive battlemented walls and the same towers (though still with squat tent roofs—the tall spires we see today were not built until the 17th century) *(Plate p. 110);* and within the ramparts rose the white walls of the churches, surmounted by the warm golden glow of their domes. At the gates the guards stood vigilant watch, and round the walls the sentries kept up their ceaseless pacing, disturbing the silence of the night with their watchwords. Within the triangle formed by the Moskva, the Neglinnaya and the moat which joined the two rivers, the Kremlin towered over the timber-built town below, casting the reflections of its massive red and white walls on the placid water. The citadel was linked with the bustling settlement which surrounded it by a number of chain drawbridges and one stone bridge; and on every side the suburbs of the town straggled out into the countryside to disappear in the distant haze.

Building continued in the Kremlin during the 16th century: streets and squares, churches and even monasteries, mansions for the Prince, the Metropolitan, the boyars, store-rooms and domestic offices. "In its extent the citadel almost resembles a city," wrote Baron Herberstein, the Emperor's ambassador in Moscow in the reign of Vasily III.

140

Muscovite painting of the closing decades of the 15th century and the early years of the 16th is inseparably bound up with the name of Dionysius (Dionisy), who ranks with Theophanes the Greek and Andrey Rublëv as one of the three great painters of mediaeval Russia.

We do not know the exact dates of Dionysius's birth or death, and can only deduce from indirect evidence that he was born not earlier than 1440 and died not later than 1505. After the latter date, at any rate, his name is not mentioned in the chronicles. Like Theophanes, he was a layman; and—in this very unlike "the gentle monk Andrey"—he can even be suspected of a tendency towards free thinking, if such a term can properly be used in relation to the mediaeval period. We learn from a contemporary that he did not observe fasts with any great rigour and that his behaviour may sometimes have fallen short of the strict requirements of the Church. It may be added that rarely has fate been so kind to an artist as it was to Dionysius: thanks to the early ripening of his talent and the help of highly placed patrons (for unfortunately talent by itself is no guarantee of success) prosperity accompanied him from his earliest years to the closing days of his life.

Dionysius is known both for his wall-painting and his icons. Contemporaries remarked on his rare fertility: for the Monastery of Joseph of Volokolamsk alone he painted no fewer than 87 icons. He worked both in Moscow and in other parts of the country on commissions from the Grand Prince and other patrons. The volume of work he undertook made it necessary for him to employ a considerable number of assistants; and in order to meet the demand for works in the "manner of Dionysius" which had achieved such popularity he had to have a staff of permanent assistants in his own "studio". And it must be admitted that it is sometimes not easy to distinguish between the work of the master and of his pupils—a fact which has created difficulties for modern experts but must have given satisfaction to the artist's customers.

Of all the works produced by Dionysius in such abundance the only ones which survive are the paintings in the Church of the Nativity of the Virgin in the Monastery of St Therapont (near the town of Kirillov in the Vologda region), done in 1500-1502 with the help of his sons Vladimir and Theodosius, who had acquired their father's manner to perfection *(Plate p. 157);* the frescoes in the Chapel of the Praises of the Virgin in the Cathedral of the Dormition in Moscow (though not all authorities accept these as Dionysius's own work); and a number of icons, two of which are signed by the artist.

An excellent example of Dionysius's style is provided by the icon of the "Crucifixion" which he painted in 1500 for the iconostasis of the church in the Pavlo-Obnorsky Monastery (now in the Tretyakov Gallery) *(Plate p. 151).*

On the rocky hill of Golgotha a black Cross bearing the crucified Christ towers above the walls of Jerusalem. Christ is dead: His head has fallen on to his right shoulder, His eyes are closed, His body hangs limp. To the left of the Cross are the Mother of God and the three Marys. Pressing her hand to her face, the Virgin stands rigid in wordless sorrow, unable to take her eyes off her dead Son. One of the women supports her tenderly, as if afraid that her strength will fail her. To the right is the Apostle John, with sorrowfully bent head and one hand pressed against his breast, as if to still the beating of his grief-stricken heart. Behind him is the Roman centurion Longinus, who

according to certain apocryphal accounts pierced Christ's side with his spear: he is gazing at the Crucified One, bending slightly backwards as if in astonishment. Above the Cross hover weeping angels. Under the arms of the Cross the angels responsible for governing the movements of the heavenly bodies are making haste to drive the sun and the moon from the sky; for in the moment when Jesus gave up the ghost "there was a darkness over all the earth... and the sun was darkened." In a dark cavity at the foot of Golgotha is a skull. This is an element almost invariably found in representations of the Crucifixion. It is Adam's skull; for one of the ancient apocryphal stories had it that the First Man was buried at this very spot, on the hill of Golgotha, and so the blood of Christ, spilling on to Adam's bones, washed away the original sin which hitherto had lain heavy on all mankind.

The clear-cut outlines of the figures and the linear rhythm of the folds in their garments convey an impression of the numbness which has seized them. The silent and motionless bystanders and the beautiful face of the Crucified One, showing no trace of the sufferings He has endured, transform this scene of martyrdom and of mourning into a solemn timeless act which takes us beyond ordinary human sensibilities. The clear luminous colours—green, pink, gold, scarlet and blue—stand out radiantly against the snow-white wall, as if the pigments had been produced by crushing precious stones to powder, reminding us that days of sorrow give place to joy, and that death is surely followed by resurrection.

This icon and other surviving works show that we do not look to Dionysius for the passionate intensity of Theophanes or the emotion of Rublëv. He is not interested in human passions, he does not seek to penetrate into the inmost recesses of the human soul. It is evident at once that he is "a craftsman of surpassing refinement", as a contemporary called him. The proportions of his figures are deliberately elongated, with small hands, feet and heads, and delicate features; their faces are handsome but unexpressive—sometimes, indeed, rather insipid. Sometimes—particularly in icons—his saints are so similar to one another that they are like twin brothers. There is never any violent movement: the whole atmosphere is one of dignity and serenity. Every stroke of the drawing suggests that God's elect know nothing of human passions, and the bright colours reinforce the mood of ceremonial elevation.

The magnificence, the solemnity and the elegance of Dionysius's

style were ideally matched to the mood of the time; for the Muscovite state was now entering its period of greatest political and cultural achievement. And as we look at Dionysius's icons or his paintings in the Monastery of St Therapont we realise why this accomplished but rather cold artist was a favourite with Ivan III and his closest adviser Iosif Volotsky, the ruthless persecutor of heretics.

The artists of the 16th century owed a great deal to Dionysius. By his many representations of the miracles and parables of Christ, which had hitherto been of rare occurrence in painting and had no established canons, he contributed to the enlargement of the subject matter and iconography of Russian art. By the same token the frontiers of religious art were extended. Nor of course must we forget the fortunate concordance between Dionysius's style and the aspirations of the period.

In the 16th century building work in stone went on all over the country. The main emphasis was on fortifications, for the Swedes and the knights of the Livonian Order were pressing on the country's western borders, and in the east and south the Tatars were again active. Accordingly the frontiers had to be defended, and all round Moscow and its outlying territory were fortified monasteries and cities like Tula, Kolomna, Zaraysk, Nizhny Novgorod, Pskov and Smolensk.

In Moscow itself there was no lack of work for builders, and craftsmen skilled in every trade were summoned from all over Russia to play their part in the Tsar's building programme. In the 1580s a special department, the Masonry Board, was established to take charge of all government building. Moreover during the struggle for the unification of the country great quantities of works of art of all kinds—icons, bone and wood carving, objects of gold and silver, and so on—were brought to Moscow from the old capitals of the feudal apanages. The flow of such material to Moscow was intensified during the reign of Ivan the Terrible (1547-1584), when it was brought in almost by the cart-load. All these factors together led to a situation in which the work of the architects, painters and other craftsmen of the 16th century gradually tended to lose the distinguishing characteristics of the local schools, which merged with the school of Moscow to produce a unified stylistic amalgam. There were, of course, still some local features: thus if we consider certain churches in the Pokrovsky Monastery in Suzdal *(Plates pp. 61-64)* or the Cathedral of the Dormition *(Plate p. 100)* in the citadel of Rostov *(Plates pp. 98-99)* we recognise the blind arcades as a reminiscence of an ancient local tradition. Nevertheless the features which immediately strike us in these and other 16th century buildings are the elements common to them all which reflect the accepted style of the period.

Among the works of fortification built in Moscow in this period mention must be made of the walls and towers of the old Kitay-Gorod, built by Petrok Maly between 1534 and 1538. These fortifications were now of vital importance to the city, for in the event of a siege of any duration the Kremlin could no longer have accommodated the greatly enlarged population of Moscow. The new fortifications, like those of the Kremlin, were designed for the new conditions of warfare based on the use of fire-arms.

The Kitay-Gorod was the business and commercial quarter of Moscow in this period, densely packed with shops and craftsmen's workshops. It was in this area that Ivan the Terrible later built the first timber Gostinny Dvor (bazaar). The name of the Kitay-Gorod is usually derived from the Russian name for China *(Kitay)*, but in fact there is no basis for this etymology. *Kitay* comes from an old Russian word meaning "wattle", and we have already noted that the word for "town", *gorod*, originally meant a fortress. A year before the erection of the stone wall round the Kitay-Gorod we find the following passage in the chronicles: "A fortress was built in Moscow, made of earth; ... most skilfully was it constructed ... Slender branches were woven round a stout log; within this,

156

earth was built up and ... firmly established ... And they gave the fortress the name of Kitay." And so the name which at first sight appears so exotic finds a simple and natural explanation.

As we have seen, the monasteries played an important part in the defence of the country. Of those in the area round Moscow the most important are the Novodevichy and the Monastery of the Trinity and St Sergius.

The Novodevichy Monastery *(Plates pp. 152-153)* was built in 1524-25 by Vasily III in fulfilment of a vow he had taken in 1514, before undertaking a campaign against Smolensk; and accordingly the principal church in the monastery—a five-domed structure built in brick with stone details, following a typical 16th century pattern—was dedicated to the icon of Our Lady of Smolensk *(Plate p. 155)*. The monastery was built at a bend in the River Moskva, at a point where there were three crossings, leading respectively to Dorogomilovo, Krymsky Brod and the Vorobyëvy Gory ("Sparrow Hills"). The site selected for this new monastery was a clear indication of its strategic importance; and we are reminded of this at once by the great machicolated walls and towers, decked out though they now are with a tracery of stone ornament added in the 17th century *(Plate p. 154)*. Indeed this decoration, like the airy openwork silhouette of the belfry, the elegant red and white refectory church, and the church above the entrance gateway with its decorative domes and carved scallop-shells—all built in the 17th century in the style known as "Naryshkin baroque"—merely serves to emphasise the massive bulk of the old 16th century fortifications.

The Monastery of the Trinity and St Sergius also stood on one of the approaches to Moscow. Founded by Sergy Radonezhsky in the middle of the 14th century and originally built in timber, it was burned down by the Tatars in 1408. It was then rebuilt, again in timber—of which there was an abundant supply in the dense forests which stretched for many miles round the monastery. For several decades the only stone building here was the Cathedral of the Trinity (1422) *(Plates pp. 149-150)*. It was not until 1469 that a second stone building was erected, the refectory church (reconstructed in the 17th century); then, eight years later, craftsmen from Pskov built in brick the small single-domed Church of the Holy Ghost *(Plates pp. 158-159)*.

It might be thought that the bitter experience of the preceding hundred and fifty years had shown the prime importance of having secure fortifications. Yet a beginning was not made until 1540, and even then there was no great air of haste: the stone ramparts which replaced the old timber palisades were fully ten years in the building. Once built, however, the stout battlemented walls and massive towers with their squat tent roofs served their purpose well. In 1608, for example, in the evil days of the *Samozvanshchina*, the "Time of the Impostors" or Time of Troubles—the "Ruin of Moscow", as the old historians called it—the Monastery of St Sergius successfully withstood many months of siege by Polish and Lithuanian forces.

During this period church building continued actively, as in the past. Perhaps the most important monastery church dating from this time is the Cathedral of the Dormition in the Monastery of the Trinity and St Sergius, which was begun in 1559, in the reign of Ivan the Terrible, but not completed until 26 years later *(Plates pp. 166-167)*. Built in brick, with a vaulted roof, five domes and five apses—

the present hipped roof with massive onion domes dates from a later period—it somewhat resembled the Cathedral of the Dormition in the Kremlin. Thus both in plan and in architectural form the Cathedral of the Dormition in St Sergius was a wholly traditional building.

A very distinctive type of church which now made its appearance, however, was the "tower church" with its striking tent roof. One of the first of these was the Church of the Ascension built in 1530-32 in the village of Kolomenskoe, an estate belonging to the Grand Prince in the countryside near Moscow *(Plate p. 162)*.

Apart from the fact that the Kolomenskoe church is built in brick with stone detailing in the normal 16th century manner, the building represents a striking departure from the accepted standards of stone-built church architecture, with the tiered structure of its tower, the octagonal tent roof surmounted by a small lantern and cupola, the high basement with a gallery and steps running down to ground level, and the absence of an apse, a feature hitherto included in all stone-built churches. "Made in the image of a church built in wood," the people of Moscow very rightly decided; and they added, struck with admiration at the builders' skill: "Such a church had never been seen in Russia before."

No doubt the admiration of contemporaries for the church at Kolomenskoe encouraged the architects of the day to further efforts in the same direction. Numbers of other tower churches were now built, in designs of increasing complexity. In the Church of the Decollation of St John the Fore-runner (1547) in the village of Dyakovo, on the outskirts of Moscow, the central tower is surrounded by four smaller corner towers; and the Cathedral of the Protection of the Virgin "on the Moat", in Red Square in Moscow, has no fewer than nine towers.

Few people will recognise this interesting building under its original name, but it is widely known as the Cathedral of St Basil the Blessed. Basil the Blessed was a *yurodivy*, a "witless one", who apparently died in Moscow in 1552, the year of the capture of Kazan. He had become famous for his fearless denunciation of the cruelties of Ivan the Terrible—for in those days it was thought that the simple-minded enjoyed the special favour of God and that even the Tsar could not compel them to keep silent. Basil was buried in the churchyard of the Trinity Church, which stood on the site later to be occupied by the Church of the Protection. He was canonised soon after his death, and when the cathedral was built one of the internal chapels was dedicated to him; but the saint was so popular in Moscow that the whole cathedral came to be known as the church of Basil the Blessed *(Plate p. 169)*.

The Church of the Protection was built in fulfilment of a vow. In mediaeval Russia important events were not commemorated by the erection of monuments but by the building of churches; and the new cathedral was built to celebrate the capture of Kazan from the Tatars. Kazan fell on 1st October 1552, on the feast of the Protection of the Virgin, and this determined the dedication of the cathedral.

The chronicler gives a concise description of the architecture of the cathedral in these words: "A church was built of most wondrous form, having nine altars of various appearance and form erected on a single base". And indeed, as we can see today, the nine towers rise from a single platform, the central tower having a tent roof with a small bulbous dome, the others onion-shaped domes ribbed and fluted in varying patterns, so that no one of the towers is exactly similar to any of the others. The

164

different towers are linked by a gallery with with staircases and flights of steps which runs round the entire building. (The flights of steps, the galleries and the belfries were added in the 17th century). Here and there the brick walls are relieved by the gleam of coloured tiles; the foundations, the basement and the architectural details are in stone.

According to an old legend Ivan the Terrible caused the builders of the cathedral, Barma and Posnik, to be blinded so that they should never build another church to compare with it. Whether true or not, this grisly tradition does at any rate show the impression made on contemporaries by the fantastic architecture of St Basil the Blessed.

In the reigns of Ivan the Terrible's successors, Fëdor Ivanovich and Boris Godunov, building continued in the principal cities of Russia. In the 1590s Fëdor Kon built the citadel of Smolensk. In Moscow two further defensive lines were constructed, the "White City" and the "Earthen City", and the dominance of the Kremlin was still further enhanced by the heightening of the bell-tower of Ivan the Great (1600). The appearance of the streets of Moscow was also now transformed. The citizens were no longer exposed to the risk, in rainy weather, of sinking up to their knees in mud: the streets in the centre of the town were paved with wood, and even in the lesser streets planks were provided on which pedestrians could pass safely over the mud and slush. The people of Moscow were sure that there was no fairer city in all Russia: "Majestic and beautiful is this mighty city"— such was the proud boast of its citizens.

To bring to life the vanished world of the Middle Ages on the basis of the fragments which have survived from the past is a well-nigh impossible task. Wars, ignorance and indifference, and the ruthless destruction of antiquities have caused irreparable loss and damage. Thus our knowledge of the monumental painting of the 16th century depends mainly on descriptions by contemporaries, together with a few fragments of actual painting which have miraculously survived. We must now consider what account can be given of this painting on the basis of the scanty material available to us.

The artists now tended to make increasing use of Old Testament subjects drawn from various edifying collections and from the lives of Russian saints. No definite canons had yet been laid down for these subjects, and the nature of the themes made it possible for the artists to introduce all kinds of lively and entertaining details. The spirit of the times was expressed in the russifying of the Gospel

165

stories: thus a publican and a Pharisee are shown praying in front of an icon of the Saviour, the miracle of the healing of the man born blind takes place in a single-domed Russian church, and so on. In church paintings dating from the reign of Ivan the Terrible we can detect a preference for apocalyptic themes, understandable enough in that period of trial and tribulation. The Tsar's lowering glance drove away the luminous images created by Andrey Rublëv, Dionysius and their followers; in their place representations of the Last Judgment painted detailed pictures of the torments of Hell (as in churches in the Aleksandrova Sloboda, Yaroslavl and Solvychegodsk), and the churches of the 16th century became tenanted by hosts of winged demons.

In the reign of Ivan IV the Golden Room in the Kremlin Palace was decorated with painting, and in Boris Godunov's the Palace of Facets. We know what these paintings were like from a description by the 17th century artist Ushakov, who was given the task of restoring them. From Ushakov's account it is clear that the paintings in both of these palaces were conceived for a particular purpose: in the phrase of a student of early Russian art, "the figures and incidents depicted were used to present certain specific ideas". The paintings were intended as a celebration of the kingdom of Russia, a glorification of the Grand Princes and Tsars and of the policies they pursued.

In this connection it is interesting to recall a curious incident which took place in 1551. In that year a council of Church leaders, the Stoglav or "Hundred-headed Assembly[2]", was held in Moscow, presided over by Ivan the Terrible himself. The assembly was concerned not only with ecclesiastical matters but with questions relating to art—what themes artists should handle and how they should represent them. The Tsar asked, for example, whether the figures of ordinary mortals who were still alive could appear on icons along with the figures of saints. The Church fathers replied that this had been the practice in ancient times and cited examples, adding that "in icons of the Day of Judgment...

there appear the figures not only of saints but of unbelievers." Although the question was direct enough, the reply was exceedingly evasive. Nevertheless it was sufficient; for within a few years there appeared the painting of the "Great Entrance" in the church of the Monastery of Sviyazhsk, which included figures of Ivan IV and Germanus, abbot of the monastery, and the icon of "The Church Militant" (originally known as "The Blessed Army of the Heavenly King"), in which, amid angels and saints, we again see the figure of the overweeningly ambitious Tsar. The icon shows the victorious host advancing in three columns along the banks of a river winding between densely wooded hills *(Plates*

167

pp. 170-173). Behind them is the city of Kazan, in flames, and in front is the Heavenly City of Jerusalem. At the gates of Jerusalem are the Virgin and Child, and angels are crowning the victors with golden crowns which they have received from the hands of Jesus. At the head of the army is the Archangel Michael, galloping along on a winged horse and pointing to the walls of Jerusalem, as if drawing attention to the celestial bliss which lies so close at hand. Behind him is the youthful commander of the army, Tsar Ivan, riding at a steady pace and looking round at the ranks of warriors behind him, while angels crown him with a golden crown.

The icon was painted to commemorate the capture of Kazan. But why, one may well ask, do the warriors include a gigantic figure of Constantine the Great carrying a cross, as well as the three princes, Vladimir, Boris and Gleb? What connection can this event which took place in the year 1552 have with a 4th century Greek Emperor and these 11th century Russian princes? There is, of course, no connection at all. The figures are included to emphasise certain historical parallels: Constantine contended with heretics, Vladimir baptised the heathen, Ivan IV converted Mohammedans to the Orthodox faith. Moreover the icon presents in pictorial form the idea, so dear to the heart of the rulers of Moscow since the time of Ivan's grandfather, of a direct line of succession running from Constantine to Vladimir, and from Vladimir to Ivan IV. And finally Boris and Gleb appear on the icon as the patron saints of the Russian army.

The trends we have noted in the painting in the Kremlin palaces and in the icon of the "Church Militant" were so strongly entrenched in this period that they are found even in works of applied art. Of particular interest from this point of view are the carved wooden reliefs on Ivan the Terrible's throne in the Cathedral of the Dormition in the Kremlin. The throne stands under a tent-shaped wooden canopy borne on four carved columns, which in turn rest on four symbolic animals. The sides of the throne are decorated with carvings of scenes, part historical, part apocryphal, showing the life and achievements of Vladimir Monomakh, from his legendary campaigns in Thrace to the equally fantastic story of his receiving the Imperial regalia from Byzantium. "Moscow, the Third Rome": the object of all this is transparently clear, particularly if we recall that the throne was made in 1551, at the very time when Ivan the Terrible was so insistent in seeking confirmation of his royal authority.

Ivan IV's reign, full of storm and stress as it was, also provided the conditions for the emergence of other and very different trends. It was a time of intense intellectual activity, when men with a bent for observation, and for drawing deductions from what they observed, sought to distinguish the elements of good and evil in human life and to establish their causes. The evil, of course, was evident at every turn; and the best minds of the day thought that once the distempers of society had been exposed it was possible to point to the means of cure. This feeling gave birth to a great body of moralising literature —of what might, in modern terms, be called propaganda. This usually took the form of stories or parables, for the 16th century was inordinately fond of the language of allegory—and in any event there were dangers about saying certain things directly. The life and behaviour of the clergy were attracting increasing attention from the enlightened thinkers of the 16th century: in particular, men remarked on the enormous increase in the wealth of the Church and on its ambition to play a part

in the government of the country. To make matters worse, although there were among the clergy men of culture and intelligence whose life was governed by the strictest rules of morality, the middle and lower clergy, particularly the monks, fell far short of these standards, being noted for their persistent drunkenness and debauchery, their greed and their hypocrisy.

Surprising as it may seem, the reaction against such conditions was sometimes expressed in the works of the icon-painters. As instances of this we may take the icons of the "Vision of the Ladder" and the "Parable of the Lame Man and the Blind Man" (both in the Russian Museum).

The "Vision of the Ladder" *(Plate p. 148)* is associated with the name of a learned monk of the 7th century, John Climacus, who was at one time abbot of the famous monastery on Mount Sinai. He received the name John Climacus, John of the Ladder, from the book he wrote called the "Ladder to Paradise"—a guide to the monastic life, which he saw as a steady ascent up the ladder of self-improvement. In the icon we see on the left the saintly author reading his work to the assembled brethren, and on the right, as if in illustration of his words, a ladder leading up from earth to Heaven, to the very gates of Paradise. At the entrance to Paradise we see Christ, the Virgin, and St John the Forerunner, along with angels; and close by, on elegantly patterned clouds, are a host of the blessed. A number of monks are engaged in climbing up the ladder. Only one of them has reached the top, and round his head glows a golden nimbus. The rest are either clinging to the lowest rungs or, having progressed half-way up, have missed their footing and, to the delight of the demons who are hovering nearby, are falling into the yawning mouth of Hell which lies below, where the rulers of the underworld, Pluto Proserpine, with all their hellish train, are awaiting their prey. The moral is so obvious that no further commentary is required.

The interpretation of the "Parable of the Lame Man and the Blind Man" is more complex *(Plate p. 147)*. We see two beggars, a lame man and a blind man, sitting at the gates of a garden: the owner of the garden, Christ, has taken pity on them and set them to watch over his property. But the wretched pair feel no sense of gratitude, and we see the blind man taking the lame man on his shoulders so that he can pluck the fruit from the trees. For this offence they are driven from the garden and, pursued by the Archangel Michael with his spear, fall straight into Hell. The blind man and the lame man are the unrighteous pastors whose duty it was to preserve the teachings of Christ in their purity—the fruits of the heavenly garden—but who had been blind and deaf to the Word of God and lame in performing the duties laid upon them. Forgetful of all spiritual blessings, they are concerned only to amass the good things of this world. There is a direct allusion here to the Church's pursuit of worldly riches, its disregard of the principles of the Gospel teaching; and the icon is thus a direct expression of the ideas which were exercising Russian society in this period.

The range of subject matter of the icons of the 16th century was enormously enlarged in comparison with earlier periods. Themes such as "In Thee rejoiceth every creature" and "Let everything that has breath praise the Lord" become increasingly frequent *(Plate p. 146)*. The denizens of Heaven are surrounded by accurate representations of plants, flowers and trees, and a variety of creatures—furred, feathered or clad with scales—such as have never existed on land or in the sea. It is as if the artists had noticed for the first time that the world was not inhabited solely by saints and incorporeal beings. It is significant that icons devoted to the lives of saints—which had occurred since the 14th century but had been relatively rare—should now begin to appear in considerable number. In these works the centre of the icon is occupied by a particular figure or figures, while round the edge is a series of square panels representing scenes from the life of the principal character. These marginal pictures are usually most entertaining and full of fascinating detail from everyday life. Moreover, in accordance with a trend which we have already noted as typical of the period, the local colour in these scenes is very Russian: the action takes place in Russian churches or palaces, the Biblical characters are frequently clad in the garb of Russian Tsars or boyars, and so on *(Plate p. 90)*.

The world of everyday reality is even more frequently represented in the miniatures than in the icons. The miniaturist enjoyed more freedom in depicting this world than the icon-painter, for he was less closely bound by traditional models: indeed, it was not easy to find models for the themes with which the miniaturist was concerned.

Among the miniatures which have survived from this period—and in this respect the miniatures have been more fortunate than the frescoes of the 16th century—the most interesting are those in the "Illustrated Collection of Chronicles" and in various lives of saints.

The "Illustrated Collection", a work commissioned by the Tsar himself, was first conceived in the 1550s and brought to completion in the 1570s. It contained all the old chronicles of the various feudal princedoms, including in particular the Princedom of Moscow, and comprehended the whole history of the world as it was then understood, from the Book of *Genesis* to the events of the 16th century. As it has come down to us, the work consists of six volumes devoted to the history of Russia and contains something like 10,000 miniatures on a great variety of subjects, which tell us a great deal about mediaeval weapons, domestic equipment, dress, and many other aspects of mediaeval life.

Many of these pictures of everyday life are found illustrating the lives of Russian saints. They show us the icon-painter at work, the monastery school, and a great variety of people going about their everyday occupations—bakers, carpenters, ploughmen, woodmen, and so on—and thus form a source of inestimable value for the social historian. There are also many pictures of quite a different type—idyllic scenes which express a deep love for the unpretentious beauties of the countryside of northern Russia. We see, for example, hermits building timber huts on the fringe of a forest, or monks engaged in earnest conversation as they stroll under an overhanging canopy of birches or firs or along the banks of a placid stream.

In the 1550s, too, following the example shown by Ivan Fëdorov, deacon of the Church of St Nicholas in the Kremlin, come the first printed books, and with them the technique of woodcut illustrations. This technique was used for headings and tailpieces, ornamental frames round the pages, and portraits of the authors—thus taking over the whole of the field which had formerly belonged to the miniaturist. There is one exception to this: woodcuts are rarely used in the 16th century to illustrate the text, though in the following century they are widely employed for this purpose. The popularity of the woodcut is hardly surprising, for it was very much quicker to engrave a picture on a block of wood, coat it with black ink and print it than to paint a picture with fine brushes on parchment—quite apart from the fact that the same block could be used to produce a large number of prints. Although it took several decades to complete the change-over, the introduction of printing meant the end of the ancient art of miniature-painting.

Surprising though it may seem, the development of the woodcut spelt the ruin of the whole of the representational art of the Middle Ages; for—slowly, perhaps, but none the less surely—it undermined the whole foundations of this art. Woodcuts, even when they depicted a particular subject or incident, were, after all, no more than book illustrations, and the prescriptions of the Church ceased to apply. Moreover the first woodcuts, like the whole technique of engraving on wood, came to Russia from the West, where the problems now presenting themselves to Russian artists had long since been solved. It was no accident, therefore, that it was the wood-engraver rather than the painter who first concerned himself in Russia with such questions as the proper representation of space or the anatomically accurate depiction of the human figure; no accident that it was the woodcuts rather than the icons which first showed the new trend, in which ordinary men and women began to replace the saints, and the scenes in which they appeared began to break free from the rules laid down by the Church. Thus the Russian woodcut of the 16th century leads directly into the art of the 17th century, the final century of the older Russia, with all its new, complex and conflicting problems.

NOTES

[1] Lavra, the Greek *laura*, originally meant a monastic community the members of which, although belonging to the same establishment, lived independently of one another. Later the term was applied in Russia to the largest and richest monasteries.

[2] In mediaeval Russia the word *nemtsy* (Germans) was applied to all foreigners, whatever their nationality. The Russian word is connected with the adjective *nemoy*, meaning "dumb" — i.e., one who could not speak Russian.

[3] "Polsky" does not mean Polish, as might be thought, but comes from *pole*, a field: the town stood amid fields.

[4] The name Volotovo is thought to be derived from the name of the pagan Slav god Veles or Volos (cf. p. 83), whose shrine seems to have stood on this spot in earlier days. The practice of building churches on the sites of former pagan temples was commonly found in the early Middle Ages not only in Russia but in western Europe.

[5] The term "hundred-headed" derives from the fact that the decisions of the assembly were later published in a collection which contained a hundred "heads" or chapters.

LIST OF ILLUSTRATIONS

182

CONTENTS

185

PRINTED IN SEPTEMBER 1967
ON THE PRESSES OF NAGEL PUBLISHERS, GENEVA

THE BINDING WAS EXECUTED
IN THE WORKSHOPS OF NAGEL PUBLISHERS, GENEVA
PLATES IN BLACK AND WHITE AND IN COLOUR
ENGRAVED BY CLICHÉS UNION, PARIS

THE PUBLISHER'S LEGAL DEPOSIT NUMBER IS 441

PRINTED IN SWITZERLAND